THE EVERYTHING KIDS'®

Pirates Puzzle and Activity Book

Set sail into a treasure-trove of fun!

Beth L. Blair & Jennifer A. Ericsson

Adams Media

Avon, Massachusetts

An Everything® Series Book.
Everything® and everything.com® are registered trademarks of F+W Publications, Inc.

Published by Adams Media, an F+W Publications Company
57 Littlefield Street, Avon, MA 02322. U.S.A.
www.adamsmedia.com

ISBN 10: 1-59337-607-3
ISBN 13: 978-1-59337-607-9

Printed in the United States of America.

J   I   H   G   F   E   D   C

This publication is designed to provide accurate and authoritative information with regard to the subject matter covered. It is sold with the understanding that the publisher is not engaged in rendering legal, accounting, or other professional advice. If legal advice or other expert assistance is required, the services of a competent professional person should be sought.

—From a *Declaration of Principles* jointly adopted by a Committee of the American Bar Association and a Committee of Publishers and Associations

Many of the designations used by manufacturers and sellers to distinguish their products are claimed as trademarks. When those designations appear in this book and Adams Media was aware of a trademark claim, the designations have been printed with initial capital letters.

Cover illustrations by Dana Regan.
Puzzles by Beth L. Blair.

This book is available at quantity discounts for bulk purchases.
For information, please call 1-800-289-0963.

See the entire Everything® series at *www.everything.com*.

Contents

DEDICATION

Yo Ho Ho!
Jennifer and Beth
dedicate
this book to our
Daddy-Os!

William A. Barber
(Jenny's Pirate Pop)

Alfred S. Sembrich
(Beth's Pirate Pop)

Ahoy, Me Hearties!

So ye be wantin' a little adventure in your day, eh? Well, ye've come to the right port, that's fer sure. We pirates be colorful characters!

We been sailin' the high seas since ancient times—since the first merchants started using boats to take their cargo from place ter place. Why sink me, there be pirates as long ago as 3,000 years. They use ter call us "The Sea Peoples" when we was stealin' and a burnin' and makin' trouble somethin' fierce for those Egyptians. Since then, we be hoisting sails and scoutin' out booty all over the world.

Even today, ye can find some of me maties. They be using cell phones and speedboats, but they still be pirates just the same. Shiver me timbers, we be a persistent lot!

So are ye lookin' to have some swashbuckling fun? This here book is a treasure trove of pirate puzzles for ye to plunder. Ye can crack codes and navigate mazes. Ye can weigh anchor with words, heave to with hidden pictures, or master some math. Ye might even learn a thing or two about some of me scurvy friends.

Avast! Have ye never heard of Blackbeard or Calico Jack? What sort of landlubber are ye? How about Captain Hook? Surely you know of him and how he lost his hand to the dread crocodile?!

More important...

...do ye know why Captain Hook was wantin' to cross the road?

1C	2A **O**	■	3A **G**	4D	5D	■	6F	7G	■
8G	9C	10E	■	11E	12F	13G	14E	15B	16A **D** -
17F	18F	19D	20E	■	21C	22B	23C	24C	25B **!**

Hang onto yer bilge mop 'cause this riddle be that funny! Pencil in the words that be suggested by the clues. Put the numbered letters in their proper place in the grid. Work back 'n forth 'tween the two until you be getting the answer.

A. Barking pet

$\underline{D}$ $\underline{O}$ $\underline{G}$
16 2 3

B. After nine

$\underline{}$ $\underline{}$ $\underline{}$
22 25 15

C. Not tall

$\underline{}$ $\underline{}$ $\underline{}$ $\underline{}$ $\underline{}$
21 9 23 24 1

D. Fish catcher

$\underline{}$ $\underline{}$ $\underline{}$
19 4 5

E. How much medicine to take at one time

$\underline{}$ $\underline{}$ $\underline{}$ $\underline{}$
20 14 11 10

F. Dislike very much

$\underline{}$ $\underline{}$ $\underline{}$ $\underline{}$
17 18 6 12

G. Camping bed

$\underline{}$ $\underline{}$ $\underline{}$
13 7 8

Buckets and scuppers, we almost forgot! Do ye like the idea of searchin' fer treasure? Then don't be missin' the very last puzzle in this here book—that's the one where ye gets to search for all the booty that's been hidden on almost every page.

Yo ho! *Barnacle Beth & One-Eyed Jen*

Turkish Delight?

Before he ruled the Roman Empire, a young Julius Caesar was captured by Turkish pirates and held for ransom. The pirates intended to ask for a certain amount of gold in return for his safety, but Caesar was insulted at the low price. He told the pirates to ask for more!

ARRRR! A nice, fat hostage such as yourself should bring

$$X + V + I + I + I + I + I$$

pieces of gold!

Are you nuts?! I'm worth at least

$$C - L - X + V + V$$

pieces of gold!

Use the key to Roman Numerals to add or subtract the equations. See how much gold Caesar thought he was worth!

KEY

I = 1
V = 5
X = 10
L = 50
C = 100

Funny Guy

Fill in the boxes with letters that appear three times or more. Read the remaining letters to find the answer to this silly bit of pirate history:

What pirate was famous for his practical jokes?

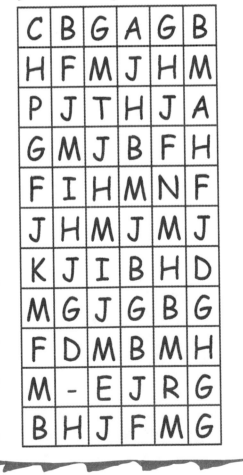

C	B	G	A	G	B
H	F	M	J	H	M
P	J	T	H	J	A
G	M	J	B	F	H
F	I	H	M	N	F
J	H	M	J	M	J
K	J	I	B	H	D
M	G	J	G	B	G
F	D	M	B	M	H
M	-	E	J	R	G
B	H	J	F	M	G

ARRRR! That's NOT funny!

Connect the dots to see the practical joke!

Buccaneers

"Buccaneers" was the name given to the pirates of the West Indies. Before they became known as pirates, buccaneers raised pigs and cows for a living. Believe it or not, their name comes from a French word that describes how they cooked their meat! Follow the directions to find the name of the recipe.

1. Connect dot 1 to dot 2.

2. Connect dot 3 to dot 4.

3. Connect dot 5 to dot 6.

4. Put your left thumb on dot A. Trace around the end of your thumb, beginning and ending on the line.

5. Repeat with dots B, C, and D.

6. Draw a circle that connects dots E, F, G, H .

KISS THE COOK

1•   3•
  A•   C•
              E•
        F•   •H
  B•   D•   5•
2•   4•   G• •6

Privateers

"Privateers" were pirates who worked for their own government. They carried special papers giving them permission to attack ships that belonged to enemies of their country. Usually, they got to keep part of the plunder. Use the clues below to figure out the name of this legal document.

Clue	
Letter 'tween D & F =	
Letter after T =	
Letter always with U =	
Letter 'fore S =	
First letter =	
Letter 'tween L & N =	
Sixth letter =	
Three letters 'fore R =	
Letter 'tween Q & S =	
One letter after D =	
Letter after S =	
Letter 'fore U =	
Fifth letter =	
Letter 'tween K & M =	

ARRRR! Did you not know that pirates are tricky? The answer reads bottom to top!

Queen's Favorite

Sir Francis Drake was an English explorer and privateer under Queen Elizabeth I. For years and years, he had his government's permission to attack and rob Spanish ships. How did his country reward his piratelike behavior? Break the Flip-Flop Code to find out.

START & END

Sir Francis Drake is also known as the first Englishman to sail around the globe! Can you find the path that leads all the way around his portrait, and back to the beginning?

Imagine living in a tiny coastal village and seeing a fleet of longboats, each packed with up to fifty warriors, heading your way. You better hide the cows, hide the food, hide the silver, and hide yourself. Better yet, just RUN, because these guys are big trouble!

Fill in the blocks to learn the name of these fierce pirates from the north. The word you uncover means "going on an overseas raid"!

Ready or Not, Here We Come!

Fill in all the squares...
...down the left sides of blocks 3, 5, 6.
...down the right side of block 5.
...down the middle of blocks 2, 4.
...across the top and bottom of blocks 2, 4, 6.

Fill in the top three blocks down the right and the left sides of block 1.

Fill in the middle square in the bottom row of block 1.

Fill in the top and bottom square on the right side of block 3.

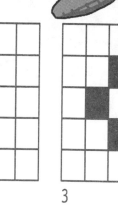

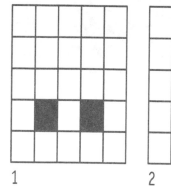

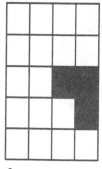

1
2
3
4
5
6

Special Effects

Edward Teach was better known as the pirate "Blackbeard." He was a big man who wore his thick hair and chest-length beard in many braids, with colored ribbons on the ends. Blackbeard also had a special trick he used to look really fierce. In fact, his appearance was enough to make many people surrender without a fight! Break the "Switch-The-Vowel Code" to learn his trick.

Bluckbaurd stock peacas if borneng, smikeng ripa ondar tha adga if hes hut!

Use markers or colored pencils to complete this portrait of Blackbeard, special effects and all!

The Barbarossa Brothers

Aruj

These brothers were considered the cruelest of pirates along the Barbary Coast in the 1500s. The galley boats they commanded depended on oarsmen, as well as sails, to move. Each oar was 15 feet long and manned by six slaves!

How many oars can you find hidden in the portraits of the brothers?

_____

What does the nickname "BARBAROSSA" mean? Break the Missing Lines Code to find out!

RED BEARD

Avast!

At one point, Aruj Barbarossa commanded a thousand pirates and twelve huge ships!

While both used the nickname, only one brother was a "barba rossa." Break the First-to-Last Code to see which one!

rujA het ldere rotherb. hizrK, het oungery, adh a eardb hatt asw rownb!

Khizr

Before becoming a pirate, Khizr helped in the family business! Follow the steps to find out his first job.

1. Write the word PIRATE.
2. Move the R to the end.
3. Change the I to an O.
4. Change the A to a T.

When Aruj died, what did Khizr do to honor his memory? Break the Vowel-Scramble Code to find out!

Ha dyad hes baurd und miostucha rad weth hannu!

A Particular Pirate

In just two and a half years "Black Bart" captured more than 400 ships, and 50 million pounds (English dollars) of treasure! Though very successful, Black Bart was a very odd pirate. He had good manners, neat handwriting, and liked classical music! He was also very particular about his clothes. To find out what Black Bart wore, look at the following list. There is one extra letter repeated in each line. Cross out the extras, and read what's left.

BCBRIBMBSBONB   WBABISBTBCOBABTB

FCFRIFMSFOFN   BFRIFTFCHFEFSF

GTHGREGE   CGORGNGERGEDG   HGAGTG

CRCEDC   FCECCATHCECRC

JSJIJLKJ   JSJAJJSJHJ
WJITJHJ   JPJIJSJTJOJJLJSJ

EDIEAEMEOENED   ECEREEOESSE

MGMOMLMDM   MCMHMMAMIMN

Avast!
Believe it or not, there was another famous Black Bart. He was a stage-coach robber in California in the 1800s!

5 x4 +4

11 -5 x4

10 +2 x2

All in the Family

When her pirate husband drowned, Cheng I Sao was elected the new chief of the "Red Flag Fleet." Ten years later, Cheng I Sao was in command of more than 1,500 ships and 70,000 pirates!

Cheng I Sao attacked every ship she came across. Which of the boats in this picture did she miss? Solve the equations on each boat. The ship that does not equal 24 got away!

5 x3 +9

3 x9 -3

4 +4 x3

11 x2 +2

6 x2 x2

9 -4 x3

11

Pirate Queens

Although there were not a great many women pirates, two of them happened to sail on the same ship! These two ladies had a whole lot in common. Find the two "extra" capital letters in each statement below. Put the first one in the space to the left of the statement. Put the second one in the space to the right of the statement. After you have collected all the letters, read them from top to bottom to get the names of these famous pirate queens.

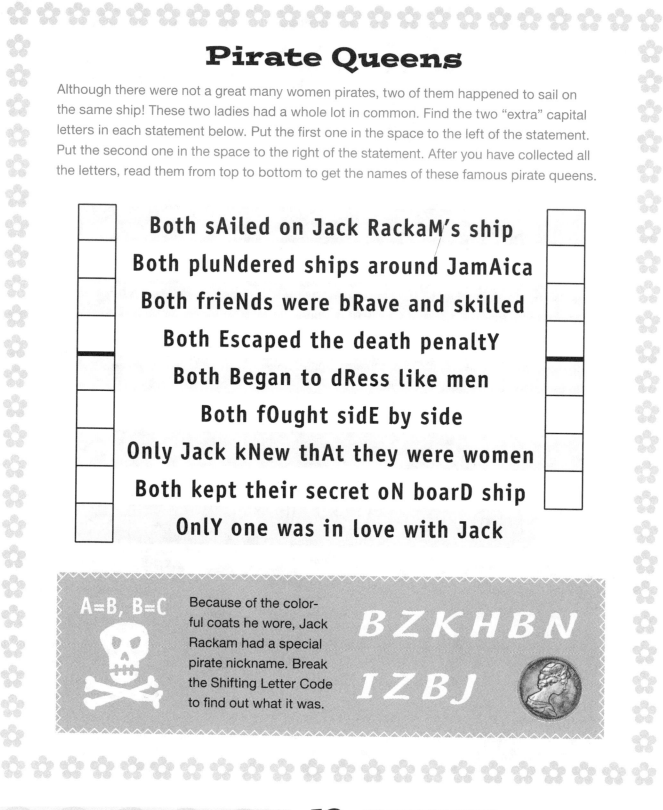

Both sAiled on Jack RackaM's ship

Both pluNdered ships around JamAica

Both frieNds were bRave and skilled

Both Escaped the death penaltY

Both Began to dRess like men

Both fOught sidE by side

Only Jack kNew thAt they were women

Both kept their secret oN boarD ship

OnlY one was in love with Jack

A=B, B=C

Because of the colorful coats he wore, Jack Rackam had a special pirate nickname. Break the Shifting Letter Code to find out what it was.

BZKHBN

IZBJ

Chapter 2

Sinister Ships

Frightful Flag

Pirates would often fly a special black flag decorated with symbols of death such as skeletons and knives. When a merchant ship saw the black flag, they knew that pirates were getting ready to attack. They would be so scared that they might surrender their gold rather than fight! Use a black crayon to color in the shapes with the letters B-L-A-C-K F-L-A-G. You'll be surprised to learn the happy sounding name of this awful omen!

HINT: If a space has no letter, don't color it in!

A Wicked Warning

Pirates tried to make their flags as frightening as possible.
Choose from the symbols below to design your personal
pirate flag. Can you think of any other scary symbols to use?

Sometimes pirates
would fly a plain
red flag—a terrify-
ing sign that they
meant to kill every-
one on board!

Draw your flag here!

Sounds Like...

A pirate ship has lots of parts! How many do you know? Try filling in all the blanks. If you get stuck, here's a hint: think of a word that fits the clue written in italics. Then, look in the word list for an answer that sounds the same!

1. The sides and bottom of a boat = H U L L
   sounds like "NOT SHINY" → DULL

2. The floor of a ship = __ __ __ __
   sounds like "QUICK KISS"

3. Tall pole that supports the sails = __ __ __ __
   sounds like "NOT SLOW"

4. The left side of the ship __ __ __ __
   sounds like "PLACE TO PLAY TENNIS"

5. Space to store the ship's cargo = __ __ __ __
   sounds like "NOT HOT"

7. Heavy piece of metal that keeps ship in place
   = __ __ __ __ __ __   *sounds like* "ONE WHO KEEPS MONEY"

8. Sheet of canvas used to catch the wind
   = __ __ __ __   *sounds like* "BUCKET"

9. Ropes that control sails = __ __ __ __ __ __ __
   sounds like "MAKING A HOLE IN DIRT"

10. Piece of wood or metal used to steer the ship
    = __ __ __ __ __ __   *sounds like* "WHERE A COW MAKES MILK"

12. Small, round window in the side of a boat
    = __ __ __ __ __ __ __ __   *sounds like* "WHERE SANTA LIVES"

BONUS: Small lookout platform high on a mast
    = __ __ __ __ __ ' __   __ __ __ __
    sounds like "ENEMY'S EXAM"

HOLD

DECK

RIGGING

~~HULL~~

PORTHOLE

MAST

RUDDER

PORT

ANCHOR

CROW'S NEST

SAIL

Nasty Knots

A large pirate ship could have several miles of rope, or "rigging," to hold up the sails, and lots more rope to tie down the cargo. That meant pirates needed to know, and use, hundreds of different kinds of knots. One wrong turn, and a sail could come crashing down, or the precious cargo could slide overboard!

Unfortunately, this new pirate has tied a terrible knot!
Follow the rope over and under to find the correct way to untie it.

Pirate's Choice

Not all pirate ships were alike. Some were small and fast. Some were larger and more powerful. Most pirates took whatever kind of ship they could steal! Which ship belongs to this impatient pirate? Use these clues to find out:

Arrr! Where's me boat?!

→ has a figurehead
→ has a black flag
→ has three cannons
→ is a schooner

Sloop = one mast

Schooner = two masts

Barque = three or more masts

Sails in the Wind

The wind has blown right through this ship's sails! See if you can put all the letter sets in their correct place to fill the holes and complete nine words that all have the letters A-I-L. Beware—some letters fit in several places!

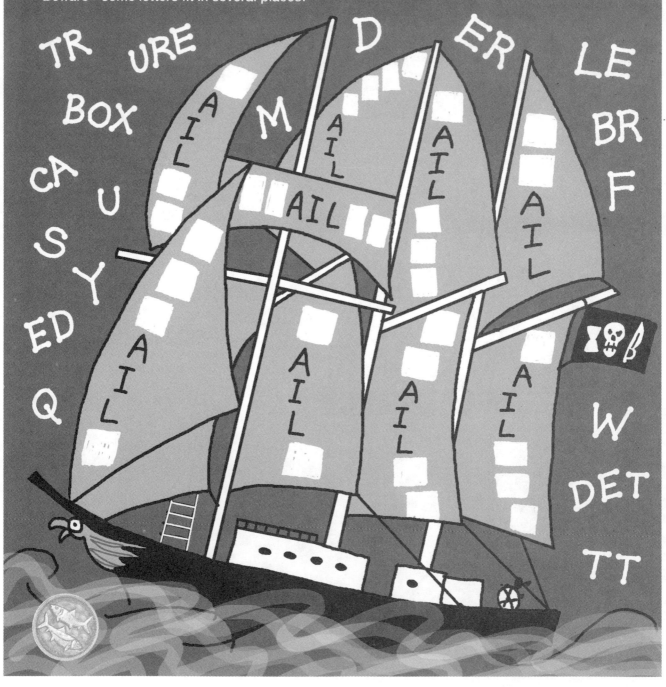

Fierce Figurehead

Since ancient times, decorations have often been put on the prow (front) of a ship. They were thought to bring good luck or to keep evil away. Figureheads might be shaped like people, animals, or imaginary creatures. Connect the dots to see what decoration the pirates have put on this ship.

WATCH OUT, MATEYS!

There are two sets of dots! One is numbered 1-85, and second set is A-Z.

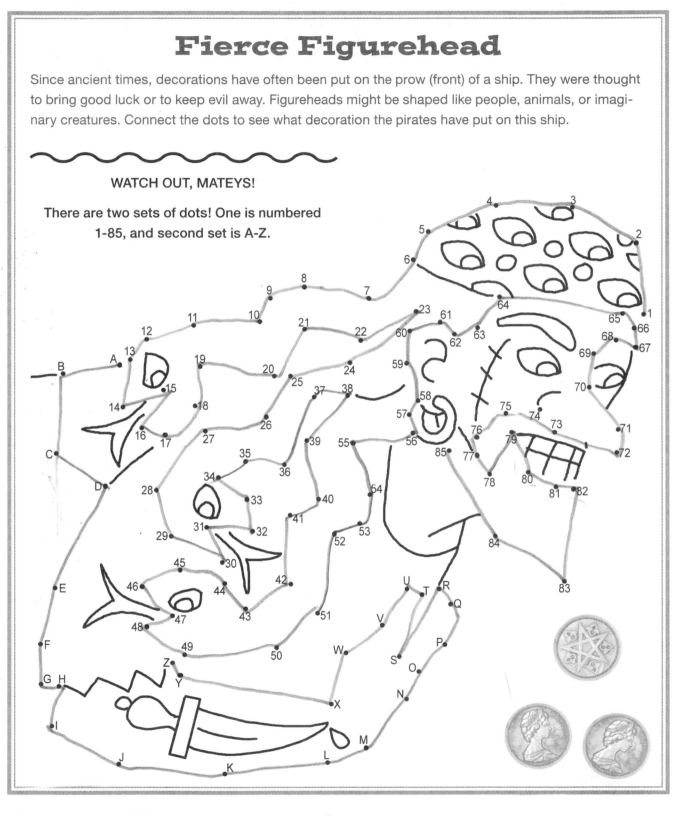

Going Up!

This pirate must climb up the ratlines to the crow's nest to get a good view. Unfortunately, he can only step in spaces where the numbers can be divided by three. Can you follow his climb to the top?

The crow's nest on a tall pirate ship might be 80 feet above the deck. That would be like climbing to the top of a six story building!

Pirate can only move forward, left or right.

7	30	1	8
8	6	11	12
12	24	9	15
4	33	8	40
15	12	6	16
9	10	32	9
30	3	21	15
28	22	24	16
4	14	6	33
9	12	2	

Going Down

A ship will stay in place once the heavy metal anchor is lowered. Four words are hiding in this puzzle that mean the same thing as anchor. Start on the left side and take one letter from each column to form a new word. Cross the letters off as you use them.

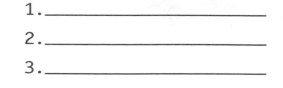

F E T A R N
S A C T E H
A T S U C E

1._____
2._____
3._____

Black Jacks

The answers to Black Jacks are two rhyming words that each have one syllable. The answer to the BONUS Black Jack has three words of one syllable.

Boat floor inspection = __ __ __ __ __   __ __ __ __ __ __

Freezing cargo space = __ __ __ __ __   __ __ __ __ __ __

Weak sheet of canvas = __ __ __ __ __ __   __ __ __ __ __

Not shiny bottom of boat = __ __ __ __ __   __ __ __ __ __

Wonderful fellow pirate = __ __ __ __ __ __   __ __ __ __ __

Cleanser for strong cords = __ __ __ __ __   __ __ __ __ __ __

Bonus: Final sail-supporting pole explosion =

__ __ __ __   __ __ __ __   __ __ __ __ __

Sneaky

Can you find the fifteen pirate ships hidden in the letter grid? Look for:

3 SCHOONERS

5 BARQUES

7 SLOOPS

Hint: Use a marker to highlight each boat!

```
R S S P I R E N O O H C S E
E E L E U Q R A B S R L U P
N U O O A T P E L S O Q O B
O Q O H O O I O P O R O S A
O R P P O P O I P A L R A R
H A T L E P S H B S I P S Q
C B S P I R E N O O H C S U
S L O O P A E U Q R A B T E
```

Captain Cutthroat needs a new ship, but he doesn't want to spend a lot of pirate gold to get one. Can you help him out? Think of a word that best fits each of the clues below. Write the words on the numbered lines, and then transfer each letter into the numbered grid. Work back and forth between the grid and the clues to get the answer to the riddle.

When is the best time to buy a pirate ship?

1B	2A	3A	4D		5E	6C	7B	8D	9C
	10E	11A		12C	" 13E	14D	15B	16C	"
	17A	18B		19D	20D				

A. Foot covering

$\overline{11}$ $\overline{2}$ $\overline{17}$ $\overline{3}$

B. Grape drink

$\overline{1}$ $\overline{15}$ $\overline{18}$ $\overline{7}$

C. To cure

$\overline{6}$ $\overline{9}$ $\overline{12}$ $\overline{16}$

D. Choo-choo

$\overline{20}$ $\overline{8}$ $\overline{14}$ $\overline{19}$ $\overline{4}$

E. Command to a dog

$\overline{13}$ $\overline{10}$ $\overline{5}$

Chapter 3
Pirate Style

Pirate Talk

Use the pirate dictionary to figure out what these two pirates are actually saying!

Ahoy, Matey!

Avast! Be ye scurvy lubber or be ye swab?

Swab, me matey, going on the Account.

Arrr! Ye be wanting booty then?

Aye! Booty to share with me hearties.

Ye best weigh anchor, lad. We shove off soon.

AHOY = *hello*

ARRR! = *exclamation*

AVAST = *stop*

AYE = *yes*

BEST = *better*

BOOTY = *treasure*

GOING ON THE ACCOUNT = *becoming a pirate*

HEARTIES = *shipmates*

LAD = *young man*

LUBBER = *land lover*

MATEY = *friend*

ME = *my*

SCURVY = *vile, mean*

SHOVE OFF = *leave*

SWAB = *sailor*

WEIGH ANCHOR = *prepare to leave*

YE = *you*

National "Talk Like a Pirate Day" is celebrated (for fun) every year on September 19th. Arrr!

Is He a Pirate?

This list will help you figure out if that nasty character you see slinking down the pier is a pirate. Finish each of these sentences with a word that ends with I-N-K. Use letters from the bottom of the page.

A pirate...

...who wears an eyepatch can only __ _ _ _.

...is fierce; he wears black, not __ _ _ _.

...doesn't take baths, so he will __ _ _ _ _.

...isn't a nice guy; he's a rotten _ _ _ _.

...hates milk; he wants rum to __ _ _ _ _.

...has gold coins that jingle and _ _ _ _ _.

...who is stupid doesn't _ __ _ _ _

his ship will _ _ _ _.

W   ST   CL

P

DR

S   TH   F

Double Trouble

Barnacle Bill and Scurvy Dog *hate* it when landlubbers
say it's so "cute" that they look exactly alike!

Arrrr, can't ye see that there are 14 diff'rences 'tween the two o' us?!

It doesn't count that they are facing in different directions.

How could the poor pirate afford to get both of his ears pierced?

To find the answer, look carefully at all of these earrings. Some look like they are linked through each other. Others look like two earrings that overlap, but are not linked. Copy down, in order, only the letters you find inside the linked earrings.

AS — GR   IT — ON   LY — WO

RK — ED   LY — CO   ST — LE

ST — HI   TO — BE   MA — BU

NC — HA   CC — AN   DY — AN

OT — (coin)   RE — TO   EE — R!

Aye, that be a good deal!

_ _ _ _ _ _ _ _ _ _ _ _

_ _ _ _ _

_ _ _ _ _ _ _ _ _ _ !

What ARRRR Pirates Like?

Use the pictures to help choose the correct ending to every riddle. Write the answers on the lines provided.

Careful! There are extra answers!

What kind of socks do pirates like best?

ARRRR_____!

In what do pirate captains sit?

ARRRR_____!

gentina

t

tichoke

Where do pirates never go?

ARRRR_____!

m

chery

chairs

What do pirates do when they disagree?

ARRRR_____!

wrestle

What is a pirate's favorite sport?

ARRRR_____!

museums

gyles

gue

30

Hairs to You!

To solve this puzzle, place each of the letters in a column in one of the boxes directly below it, but not always in the same order! We left you a few hints. After you put each letter into the correct space, you will have the very practical answer to this question:

Some pirates wore long hair and long beards, but many chose to shave their heads and faces. Why?

Name That Pirate

What would you call yourself if you were a pirate? Here is a fun way to try out different pirate names. As many people as you want can play this game.

1. Use the ruler and pencil to divide each index card into four equal pieces. Cut them apart.

2. Write each of the following pirate words on a separate piece of card.

BLACK	SCAR	FACE	RED	BEARD	LEG
ONE-EYED	DOG	NASTY	DIRTY	BLUE	GROSS
CUTTHROAT	HEART	SILVER	WOODEN	STINKY	HOOK
NOOSE	GOLD	TOOTH	LONG	SCAR	QUICK
ROTTEN	CHEAP	HAIR	NOSE	CUT	SICK
BRAVE	CRAZY	FIERCE	WILD	NOISY	COLD

Each player should make one card that has their first name on it.

3. Turn all the cards face-down and mix them up. Each player picks two or three cards depending on how long they want their pirate name to be.

4. Read the cards you chose and add the card with your own first name at the end. You can switch the order of the words on the cards if it makes your name better. For instance, "Long Nose Charlie" sounds better than "Nose Long Charlie."

5. If you don't like the words you got, pick again until you find the perfect pirate name!

Perfect Pirate Pets

Hidden in this letter string are four types of animals that some pirates kept as pets. Use a pencil, and follow these rules to find them:

→ Each animal's name reads in order from left to right.

→ Cross out the letters as you spell each name.

→ The shadows are a clue to the animals you're looking for!

CMPOARTANRAKROETTY

1. _____ 2. _____ 3. _____ 4. _____

Filthy Stinkin' Pirates

Aye, it can get pretty smelly when you're months at sea with no fresh water or soap! To learn how pirates dealt with dirty clothes, use the following rules to cross words out of the grid below.

two letter words with A

words that rhyme with DIRT

words ending in ED

different types of shoes

AT	IT	BOOT	WAS	FLIP-FLOP
EASIER	SOAPED	TO	SQUIRT	STEAL
SKIRT	CLEAN	CLOG	CLOTHES	SCRUBBED
THAN	AM	WASH	SANDAL	AN
RINSED	DIRTY	SHIRT	CLOTHES	SLIPPER

ARRRR!
Thanks for volunteerin'
to help with me laundry!

Whose Boots?

Can you match the silly description in each boot with one of the pirate names scattered on the page?

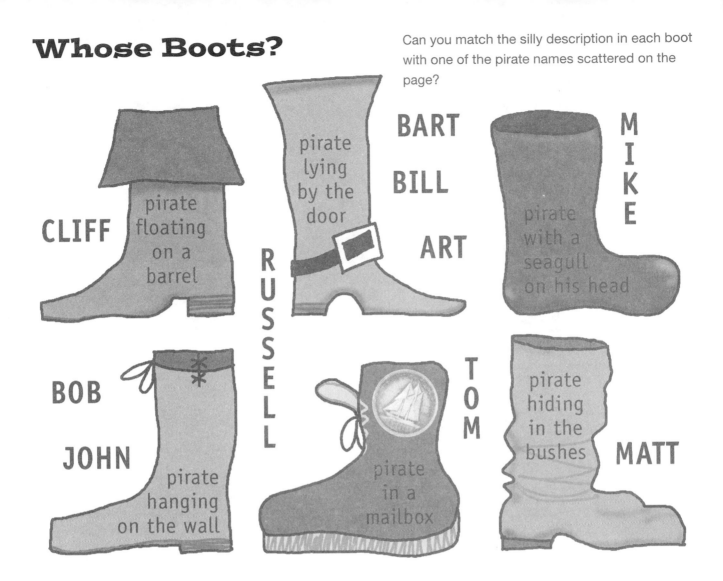

CLIFF

pirate floating on a barrel

pirate lying by the door

BART

BILL

ART

RUSSELL

MIKE

pirate with a seagull on his head

BOB

JOHN

pirate hanging on the wall

pirate in a mailbox

TOM

pirate hiding in the bushes

MATT

Captain Hook likes to wear...

...a dagger, but not a sword.
...pantaloons, but not britches.
...a pullover, but not a shirt.
...earrings, but not bracelets.

...boots, but not shoes.
...a goatee, but not a beard.
...tattoos, but not face paint.
...a parrot, but not a monkey.

Look at the words of the things that the Captain likes and figure out what they have in common. That's the secret to the Captain's style!

Dressed for Success

This pirate is ready for anything. Not only is he lookin' fierce, matey, but he's got twelve hidden daggers at the ready in case of a sneak attack! Can you find them all?

Avast!
Most pirates didn't have a lot of choice about what they wore. Like the type of ship they sailed, it often depended on what they could steal!

Chapter 4

Hard Life Aboard

What's My Line?

There was lots to be done aboard a pirate ship, and every crew member had their own responsibilities.

Look at the facing page and read what each pirate says about his job. Choose a name from the list, below, and write it by the pirate who has that job.

SAILMAKER
NAVIGATOR
SEAMAN
CARPENTER
SURGEON
COOK

Tools of the Trade

Now see if you can match the right tools to each pirate's job! Write the numbers from the list by the picture of the pirate who would most likely use those tools.

1. **NEEDLE** to sew canvas
2. **SMALL** SPOON to scoop out bullets
3. **PISTOL** for fighting
4. **SAW** to cut wood
5. **SHARP KNIFE** to cut meat
6. **HOOK** to catch fish
7. **SHARP KNIFE** to whittle pegs and plugs
8. **SCRUB BRUSH** to clean deck
9. **SHARP KNIFE** to cut skin
10. **BIG SPOON** to stir stew
11. **CUTLASS** for fighting
12. **BACKSTAFF** to measure latitude
13. **NEEDLE** to sew skin
14. **AWL** to poke holes in canvas
15. **SHARP KNIFE** for fighting
16. **SCISSORS** to cut canvas
17. **HAMMER** to pound nails
18. **COMPASS** to find North
19. **CHART** to find land
20. **SAW** to cut bone

Crowded Cargo

Pirate ships needed to have enough supplies to last at sea for months at a time. They were stuffed full with casks of water, food, rope, weapons, and lots of pirates! Ships were so crowded that many pirates slept down in the hold with the cargo. Rats liked the hold, too, because maybe they could find something to eat! Can you find the twenty-four rats hiding in with the sleeping pirates?

Awww, Cap'n, Do I Have To?

In the slow times between battles, the fierce pirate captain had to act a bit like a pirate mom—he had to get all the sulking pirates to do their chores! Fill in the blanks using words from the "treasure chest" to come up with a list of pirate jobs.

_____ DECKS
_____ BILGES
_____ RATS
_____ HULL
_____ GUNPOWDER
_____ CANNONBALLS
_____ LEAKS
_____ KNOTS
_____ TEETH

Treasure Chest

SIFT
PUMP
RETIE
SCRAPE
CATCH
SCRUB
PULL
SHINE
PLUG

AWWWK! Keep swabbin', matey!

Sea Sick

How many days have these pirates been waiting for treasure? Find all the hidden numbers in these sentences and add them up to find out!

Pirate cooks must work hard to make tender meat.

If our weight is even, the boat won't sink quickly.

As evening approaches, the south reef comes into view.

If I've got an inexpert sailor, it won't be smooth sailing.

After the sixth storm, most of our teeny sails were gone.

Fishy things to eat

S E A F O O D

Ocean plant

S E A w e e d

Peas, beans,
and peanuts

L E G o o _ _
u m e s

Space to stretch

L E G r o o m

Time of
the year

S E A s o n

Sea Legs

A sailor gained his "sea legs" when he had been onboard ship long enough to not get ill from the rolling motion of the waves. Read the clues down each of this pirate's legs. All the words in the left leg start with S-E-A. All the words in the right leg start with L-E-G.

Easy to read

L E G i b l e

Mammal
with flippers

S E A L

Mythical Story

L E G e n d

You sit
on it

S E A T

Lawful

L E G A L

How quickly can you get
your sea legs?

Yuck!

Since pirates couldn't stop at the market regularly, their food was often foul, rotten, or full of bugs. Sometimes there was no food at all! Then what did pirates eat? Read the numbered words to find an actual recipe for "Starvation Stew."

30 water.	23 smaller	8 soak.
11 stones	5 thin	28 lots
7 and	14 tender.	18 hair,
22 into	20 roast.	1 Slice
16 off	2 leather	17 the
13 make	24 pieces	9 Beat
4 into	3 knapsack	12 to
27 with	6 pieces	19 then
15 Scrape	26 serve	25 and
10 between	21 Cut	29 of

Yum!

When food was plentiful, pirates dined on a special stew made from an unusual combination of foods. Unscramble each of the ingredients, then read the shaded letters from top to bottom to find the name of this pirate "delicacy." Would you eat a bowl full of this?

SHIF = _ _ _ _

BRAC = _ _ _ _

RAGCLI = _ _ _ _ _ _

TEAM = _ _ _ _

GABBACE = _ _ _ _ _ _ _

GRINEVA = _ _ _ _ _ _ _

TRUIF = _ _ _ _ _

OONIN = _ _ _ _ _

RAHD-LOIBED SEGG =

_ _ _ _ - _ _ _ _ _ _ _ _ _ _

SCIPES = _ _ _ _ _ _

Scrub-a-Dub-Dub

Help the pirate scrub his ship from STERN (very back) to PROW (very front).

PROW

STERN

What's So Funny?

These pirates finally have a minute to relax. One pirate is telling his mate a funny joke, but they are speaking in "pirate talk." Figure out their secret language so you can share in the fun!

YOHOW HYYOHO COULD YOHON'T
YOHO THEYO HOPIR ATE
YOHO PLA YYO HOCA RDS?
YOHOBEC AUSEY OHOH
EYOHO WASYOHOS ITTIN
GYOH OON YOHO
THEYOH ODEC KYOHO!

Silly Sentences

What is happening onboard this pirate ship today? Figure out what letter can finish all the words in each sentence to find out!

Avast!
Pirates might play cards on ship, but they couldn't gamble. It was forbidden!

__razy __ooks __hop __arrots.

__ails __lap __even __illy __eagulls.

__ild __ind __hips __et __hitecaps.

__irates __ractice __lundering.

__ats __ehearse __igging __aces.

__rightening __lags __lap __itfully.

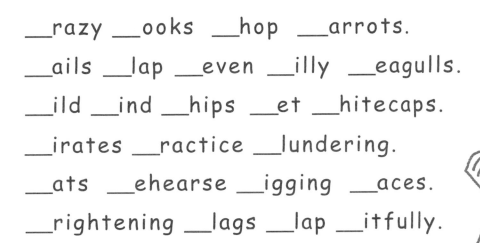

Watch Out!

There were pirates on duty around the clock to keep an eye out for enemies or other dangers. Whatever mate was on "watch" had to be alert and observant for four long hours. Pirates didn't have wristwatches, so how did they keep track of the time?

Bells were rung on the ship following this pattern:

Start of the watch: 8 bells

End of first half hour: 1 bell

Every additional half hour: add 1 bell, up to 7 bells

Start of next watch: 8 bells

This tired pirate started his watch at midnight. Draw a line from the number of bells the pirate hears to the correct time.

7 bells	*MIDNIGHT*
	12:30 AM
5 bells	*1:00 AM*
	1:30 AM
2 bells	*2:00 AM*
3 bells	*2:30 AM*
	3:00 AM
6 bells	*3:30 AM*
4 bells	*4:00 AM*

Just Knotty

ARRR!
I be
HATING
it when
that
happ'ns!

You used to be a fat landlubber, but now you're a scrawny pirate, and your pants keep falling down! You need to make a belt, but there are only scraps of rope. ARRR! What do you do?

When pirates needed to attach two pieces of rope together, they used the "sheet bend" knot. It is a strong, simple knot that they could trust not to come undone. By the time you are done making this rope belt, you will have had lots of practice tying a sheet bend!

You will need:

cotton rope about ¼ inch thick
ruler
scissors

How to make rope belt:

Cut six to eight pieces of rope, each 12 inches long. Use the sheet bend knot to connect the pieces together, one after the other. Wrap the belt around yourself before doing the last knot.

How to tie a sheet bend knot:

STEP 1:
Make a small, upside-down loop near the end of one piece of rope. Hold the loop in your left hand.

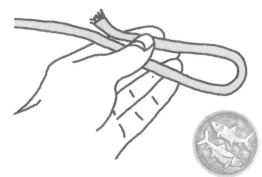

STEP 2:
With your right hand, push the end of a second piece of rope up through the loop you just made.

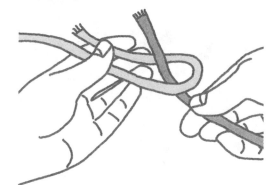

STEP 3:

Wrap the end of the second rope around and under the neck of the loop.

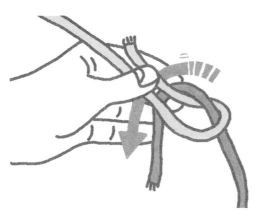

STEP 5:

Hold all four pieces of rope close to the knot and pull gently until the knot tightens.

Here's a picture of the finished knot.

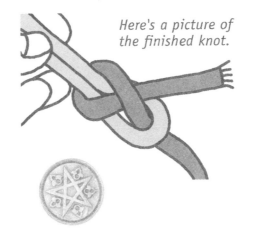

STEP 4:

Bring the end back up and slide it under itself, but not back through the loop.

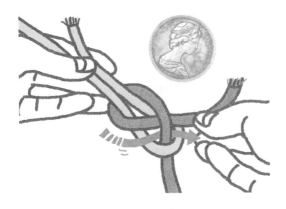

Knot Right!

Can you find the one time that KNOT is spelled correctly? Look left to right, up and down, diagonal, or even backward!

K N T O K O T K
N O N K N K T T
T T K O T O K O
O O O T N K N K
O N K K T O O N
K N O K N T O T
K O N T T N K O
N K O N O K N O

Check out **www.iwillknot.com** for a step-by-step animation of tying the sheet bend, plus twelve other knots!

Sing as You Work

Sea shanties were work songs sung by the pirates. These songs or chants had strong, simple rhythms that helped the pirates keep in time with each other. Shanties were sung especially when doing hard work, such as lifting the enormous anchor! Using the key provided, decode the lyrics to this shanty popular during the age of the great sailing ships.

Hint: Put the answer letters right over the symbols in the shanty.

Chapter 5
You're Gonna Get It

Codes of Conduct

Even though pirates were an unruly bunch, there were very strict rules of behavior they had to follow when onboard their ship. These rules were called "The Articles," and they were the same on most ships.

What were the most common rules that pirates had to obey? To find out, fill in the Alphabet Decoders below. Then figure out which code is used for each rule on the next page!

ARRRR! No one said I'd be needin' me specs to go piratin'!

Alphabet Shift (A=B, B=C, C=D)

CODE LETTERS	A	B	C	D	E	F	G	H	I	J	K	L	M	N	O	P	Q	R	S	T	U	V	W	X	Y	Z
MESSAGE LETTERS																										

Reverse Alphabet (A=Z, B=Y, C=X)

CODE LETTERS	A	B	C	D	E	F	G	H	I	J	K	L	M	N	O	P	Q	R	S	T	U	V	W	X	Y	Z
MESSAGE LETTERS																										

Number Substitution (1=A, 2=B, 3=C)

CODE NUMBERS	1	2	3	4	5	6	7	8	9	10	11	12	13	14	15	16	17	18	19	20	21	22	23	24	25	26
MESSAGE LETTERS																										

Reverse Number Substitution (26=A, 25=B, 24=C)

CODE NUMBERS	26	25	24	23	22	21	20	19	18	17	16	15	14	13	12	11	10	9	8	7	6	5	4	3	2	1
MESSAGE LETTERS																										

Rule 1:

LYVB   GSV   XZKGZRM.

Rule 5:

MN   RKDDOHMF   VGDM   NM   CTSX.

Rule 2:

MN   EHFGSHMF   ADSVDDM   OHQZSDR.

Rule 6:

ML   HGVZORMT   UILN   UVOOLD   KRIZGVH.

Rule 3:

13-12   4-12-14-22-13   12-13   25-12-26-9-23.

Rule 7:

11-5-5-16   23-5-1-16-15-14-19   3-12-5-1-14   1-14-4   18-5-1-4-25.

Rule 4:

14-15   7-1-13-2-12-9-14-7   15-14   2-15-1-18-4.

EXTRA FUN: Break this Vowel Scramble Code.

BIWURI! Briuk thi rolis und puy thi preci!

You Rule!

Now it is your turn to make up the rules. If you were the captain of a pirate ship, what would be your Articles? Everyone on your boat would have to obey them, or they could be punished. Would you make everyone eat peanut butter? Or be tickled for five minutes? You decide how serious or silly to be!

What follows is the strict and solemn code of the crew of the pirate ship

_____

(give your ship a name)

Rule 1:
_____

Rule 2:
_____

Rule 3:
_____

Rule 4:
_____

Rule 5:

Mutiny!

One of these pirates doesn't like the rules. He's planning to "mutiny" and take over control of the ship from the captain! ARRR! Who is this scurvy dog? Find the pirate with all of the following characteristics, and you'll see.

**bandana with stripes and dots
2 scars • 1 hoop earring • beard**

The Ultimate "Time Out"

What could a nasty pirate do that was so bad that other pirates would discipline him? Well, if you stole from a shipmate, refused to fight, or were too merciful to the enemy, you were in big trouble. The worst punishment was to be "marooned." That meant being left on a tiny island with nothing but a bottle of water and a pistol!

This pirate thinks he was left empty handed, but look closely—can you find the following useful items? Look for a pot, fried egg, banana, spoon, three matches, needle and thread, slice of pizza, cutlass, sailboat, drink with a straw, rope, fish-hook, slice of bacon, and a scoop of ice cream!

Poor Pirate!

A knocked-out pirate washes up on a beach. When he comes to, he can't believe his eyes! The sand is dark red. The sky is dark red. The whole island is dark red. He screams when he realizes that his skin is dark red, too! What did the pirate yell?

To solve this puzzle, think of words suggested by the clues below and write them on the dotted lines. Then fit each numbered letter into its proper place in the grid. Work back and forth between the grid and the clues.

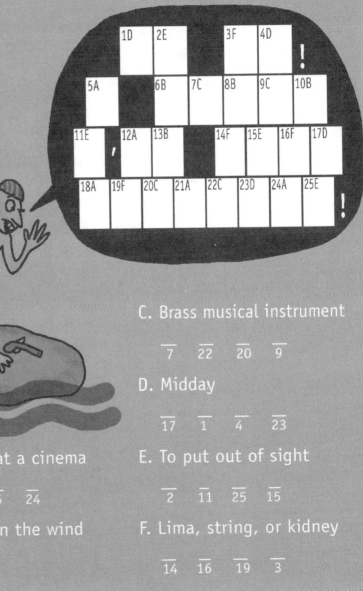

C. Brass musical instrument

‾7‾ ‾22‾ ‾20‾ ‾9‾

D. Midday

‾17‾ ‾1‾ ‾4‾ ‾23‾

A. What you see at a cinema

‾18‾ ‾21‾ ‾12‾ ‾5‾ ‾24‾

E. To put out of sight

‾2‾ ‾11‾ ‾25‾ ‾15‾

B. Toy that flies in the wind

‾10‾ ‾8‾ ‾6‾ ‾13‾

F. Lima, string, or kidney

‾14‾ ‾16‾ ‾19‾ ‾3‾

Walk the Plank

Walk the plank by replacing one letter in the word, making a new word each step of the way. You want to walk the PLANK and fall into the DRINK!

PLANK

_____

_____

_____

DRINK

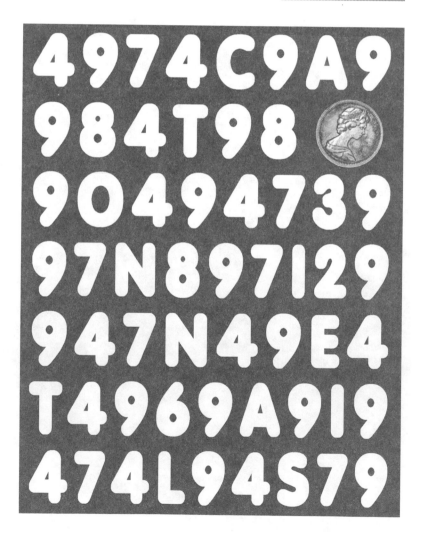

Avast!
Believe it or not, walking the plank was not a common pirate punishment. It looked good in the movies, though!

Ouch

Pirates who misbehaved were often beaten, or "flogged." A common whip was made from a piece of rope with the end unraveled. The tips of each of the nine strands were knotted to make the whip hurt even more. This nasty tool actually had a kind of silly name. Fill in all the numbers, and read the remaining letters to find out what it was.

Avast!
The pirate who was going to be beaten often had to make his own whip!

4974C9A9
984T98
90494739
97N897129
947N49E4
T4969A919
474L94S79

Double Ouch

A "bad" pirate was flogged on the bare skin of his back. That was painful enough, but after being whipped, the Captain might order another punishment. Something would be thrown on the pirate's back that would reeeeeally sting. What was it?

To find out, solve the equations along each line of this cat-o'-nine-tails. Find the line with the lowest sum, and collect the letter by the knot. Put that letter in the first space provided.

Continue collecting letters from lowest to highest sum.

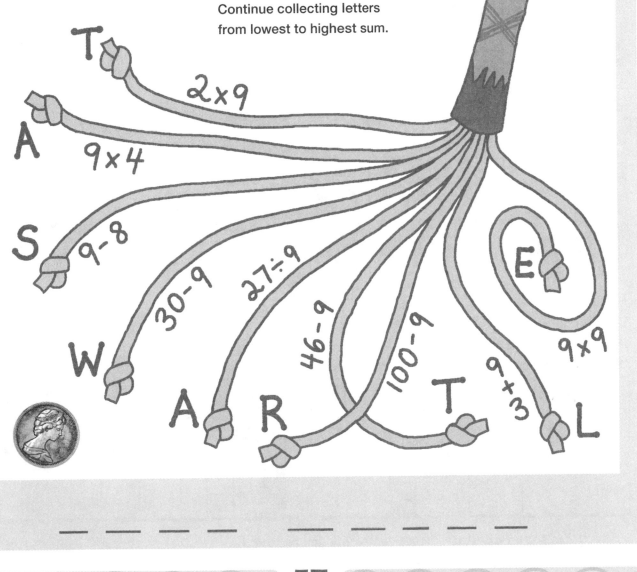

T 2×9

A 9×4

S 9−8

W 30−9

A 27÷9

R 46−9

100−9

T 9+3

L

E 9×9

_ _ _ _ _   _ _ _ _

Hanging Around

A riddle and its answer were cut up into pieces. To finish the puzzle, you must write all the letters from the scattered pieces into their proper spaces in the grid. **HINT:** Match the pattern of the black boxes.

What's the yardarm? The horizontal wooden bar that holds the sails out from the mast!

You Better Behave!

Some punishments were so awful that even a fierce pirate would think twice about breaking the rules! Complete the statements below using words from the list. Write the one capital letter from each missing word on the line at the end of the sentence. When you are done, read the letters from top to bottom to discover the name of the punishment reserved for very bad pirates!

The _____ is the backbone of the boat. ____

Your hands would be tied with _____. ____

Your _____ might be tied, too, so you can't swim. ____

The _____ of rope is passed underneath the boat. ____

Your _____ would be taken away. ____

You would be tossed _____. ____

You would sink completely _____. ____

You would be _____ under the boat. ____

And then out the other _____. ____

Your body would scrape against sharp _____. ____

Hold breath in your _____ so you don't drown! ____

Word List:

pulLed

LunGs

Underwater

sIde

barNacles

ropE

Keel

overboArd

lEgs

clotHes

Line

Brig Breakout

The brig was the prison on a ship. This pirate has been locked up a long time, but he keeps looking for a way out. Help him escape by following the correct path of B-R-I-Gs. There's a catch—you will have to figure out where the puzzle starts and ends! You can go left, right, up, and down, but not diagonally. And you must spell the complete word to get out.

Chapter 6

Avast! Attack!

Boarding Party

This pirate attack is pretty silly. How many dumb things can you find?

PIRATE

Fire Away!

This is a game for two players.

Each time you want to play, you will need ten round candies for cannon-balls, and a pair of dice.

PIRATE loads all the cannons on the left side of the page.

MERCHANT loads all the cannons on the right side of the page.

Players take turns rolling the dice. Subtract the lower number from the higher one. If the number matches a cannon's number that has a cannon-ball, the player gets to "fire away" and eat the cannonball! The winner is the player who fires all their cannons first.

Junk Jam

Fleets of pirates dominated the South China Sea during the early seventeenth century. Pirate junks (ships) looked a lot like merchant junks. It was hard to tell who was who until you were being robbed! Use the small puzzle pieces to help you locate the hidden pirates waiting to attack.

Treacherous Trick

Often pirates would fly flags from friendly countries so they could get close enough to attack a ship. This was called "flying false colors." Tricks like this made it treacherous for those who were trying to transport cargo across the seas.

Can you find ten words hiding in the word T-R-E-A-C-H-E-R-O-U-S? Look for five 6-letter words, and five 7-letter words. Write your answers on the lines below.

TREACHEROUS

Try not to use the letter S to make plurals

Hide and Seek

Spanish galleons loaded with treasure would set out from Central and South America. Before they reached the wide Atlantic Ocean, they had to sail through narrow passages between the islands of the Caribbean. It is here they were ambushed and robbed by buccaneers!

ARRR!

Complete the story using ten words containing either CC or EE. Choose words from the list, but be careful—there are more than you need!

The Spanish _____ had nowhere
                    group of boats

to _____. They were taken control of
      run away

by the Buccaneers shortly after they passed

the _____. The pirates _____
      ridge of coral   *smelled badly*

and _____, showing rotten
        made a nasty facial expression

_____. They took the treasure,
      bony mouth parts

then _____ their
        shouted with happiness

_____ _____!
  not bitter   *accomplishment*

broccoli
cheered
creeps
fleet
flee
greedy
hiccups
occupied
occured
reef
reeked
sneered
soccer
speeds
success
sweet
teeth

What POW-er!

Choose one of the corner letters in the grid. Move right, left, up, or down ONLY. When you have found the correct path, you will have spelled out the silly three-word answer to this question:

How quickly was gunpowder invented?

Hint: Use the rebus clue to help sound out the first word to look for.

Lazy Ammo

To find the silly answer to the question below, start at the letter marked with a dot. Collect every other letter until you reach the end. The trick is figuring out which way to travel around the circle!

What does a cannonball do when it isn't being fired?

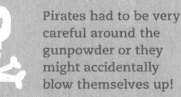

Pirates had to be very careful around the gunpowder or they might accidentally blow themselves up!

That's why one of the most dangerous jobs on a pirate ship was to be a "powder monkey." These young men ran with scoops of gunpowder from the storeroom to the gunners working the cannon!

Silly Sentences

Pirates are getting ready for a raid. What's going on? Figure out what letter can finish all the words in each sentence to find out!

__onytailed __irates __lot __oisonous __arties.

__even __loops __lide __ilently __outhward.

__rashing __annonballs __ut __ircular __raters.

__irty __an __raws __angerous __aggers.

__lways __void __bsolutely __wful __mbushes!

I Spy

Captain Dirty Dog has sailed a little too close to the ship he's sneaking up on! His spyglass (telescope) is only showing pieces of the galleon he plans to attack. Can you tell what he's looking at?

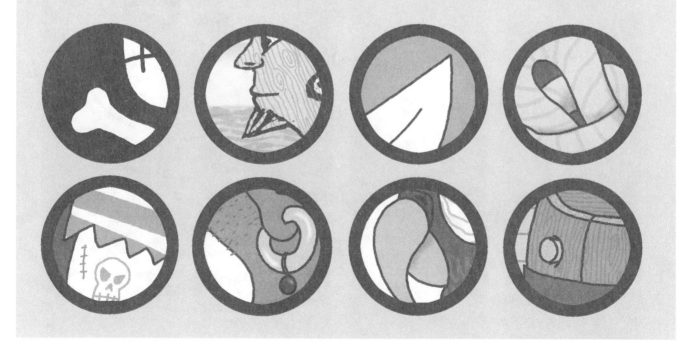

Sneaky Ship

Pirates had an advantage if they could surprise the ship they wanted to plunder.
Can you tell which of these ships is so sneaky that all you can see is its shadow?

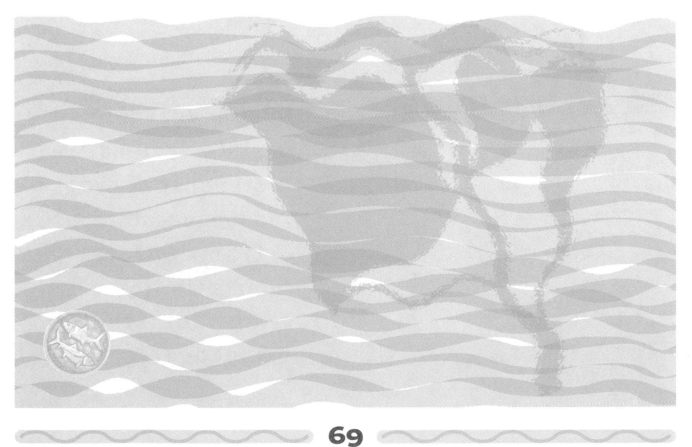

Be Afraid

Pirate attacks were designed to make the victim's knees shake. Can you find four words that mean "to frighten " hidden in this grid? Take one letter from each column moving from left to right. Each letter can only be used once, so cross them off as you use them.

S	L	A	C	K
S	H	O	R	E
A	H	O	R	E
P	C	A	I	M
S	A	N	R	C

Scared Ya!

As a pirate ship approached its prey, the attacking pirates would act wild and crazy. Often the crew of the ship under attack would be so scared, they would give up without a fight! There's a special word for when pirates acted out like that. To learn what it is, remove the extra letter from each crazy behavior in the list, and place it on the line. Then read the letters from top to bottom.

___ vdavncveavrouvnd
___ yaelalavioalenatlya
___ pwapvepspwoprdps
___ roudoegoesotuoroes
___ srtramrprfrererrt
___ iscirieaimiloiudily
___ fninrnepnistnolsn
___ gmagkgegfagcegsg

Get a Grip

Pirates threw a grapnel, or grappling iron, onto the ship they were attacking. The hooks got caught in the rigging and made it easier for the pirates to pull the ship close so they could jump on board! Can you find your way through this tangle from START to END?

START

END

Direct Hit

Which cannon made which holes in the side of this ship? Add all the numbers along each path, including the number in the cannonball. The odd numbered paths are direct hits!

Avast!

Pirates would throw many nasty things at a ship they were attacking: smoky "stinkpots" caused gagging and coughing; pointy "caltrops" got stuck in the crew's feet; and explosive "grenados" created damage and confusion.

Chapter 7
Plunder and Booty

Whose Treasure?

Some of the signatures of the most famous pirates have been discovered on scraps of their treasure maps. Unfortunately, the parchment is so old that only part of their name is still readable. Using the list provided, can you decide which pirates' maps have been found?

Sir Francis Drake

Sir Henry Morgan

Captain Kidd

Black Bart

Calico Jack

Anne Bonny

Mary Read

Blackbeard

Jean Laffite

Cheng I Sao

What to Take?

Gold and jewels were not the only treasures pillaged by pirates. They took anything that could be used or sold from a ship, including the ship itself! Think of a word that goes with each clue, and fit them into the numbered puzzle grid. We've left you some B-O-O-T-Y to get you started, plus some of the answers scrambled.

WECR   TREAW   SCIPES
FEFEOC
PORE   DOOF
ATE   GLOD
EBER
ROVIY   LASSI   PHIS

ACROSS

2. Dried leaves to smoke
5. Plain liquid to drink
8. Canvas sheets
11. Drugs to treat sickness
12. Precious metal (yellow)
14. What you wear
15. Makes food tasty
18. Men who run the ship
19. Gems to wear

DOWN

1. Strong cords
3. What you eat
4. Strong drink from fermented grapes
5. Stuff to fight with
6. Leaves used to brew a hot drink
7. Liquor made from molasses

8. Vessel to sail in
10. Captive people forced to work
13. Fizzy drink made from malt and hops
14. Dried beans used to brew a hot drink
16. Precious bone
17. Precious metal (grey)

Captain Crafty's Secret Stash

Captain Crafty hid all of his treasure on his island. After Crafty was killed, his crew went looking for it. These pirates knew several things about their captain that helped them decide which hiding place the captain used!

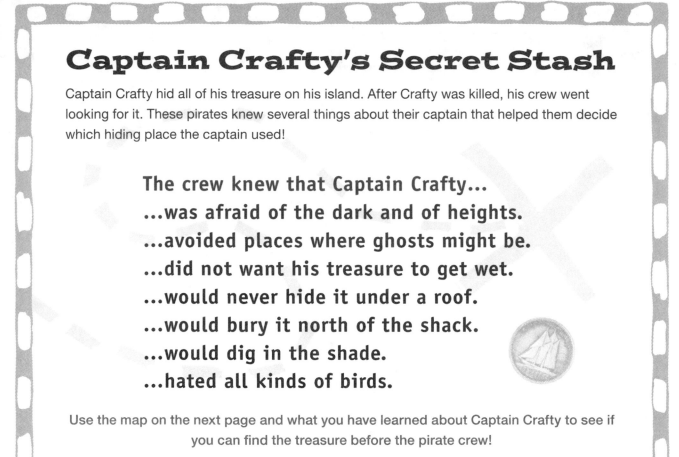

The crew knew that Captain Crafty...
...was afraid of the dark and of heights.
...avoided places where ghosts might be.
...did not want his treasure to get wet.
...would never hide it under a roof.
...would bury it north of the shack.
...would dig in the shade.
...hated all kinds of birds.

Use the map on the next page and what you have learned about Captain Crafty to see if you can find the treasure before the pirate crew!

Hidden Treasure

This grid looks like it is chock full of treasure, but look carefully. There is only one time that the word is spelled out correctly. Can you find it?

```
E T R E S R E T R A E S U T
E R T R E T E U T A U T R R
T E T E R U T R A E S T E E
R A R S T R R R U T R U T S
E S E T R E E S S S R T R U
A R U S T A A E T U A A E R
S E R T R A S S U R E E S E
U T E E R S U E R T T E R S
R R T T U E R R E E U R E T
```

Booty-ful!

This beautiful gem contains the names of several jewels and precious metals. See how many kinds you can form by using only letters that are attached to each other. Circle the ones in this list that you can find:

amber   emerald

gold   sapphire

silver   topaz

diamond   pearl

ruby

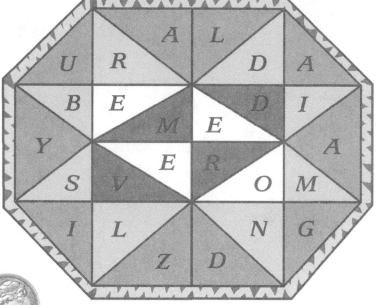

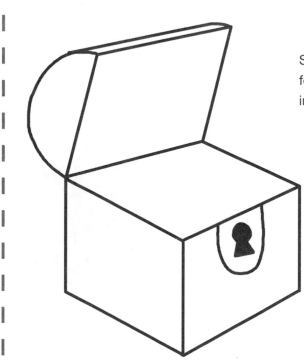

Fill 'er Up!

Stare at the spot between the black jewel and the coin for thirty seconds without blinking. Now look at the inside of the empty treasure chest. What do you see?!

Real Treasure?

We left you a few hints—which is more than a pirate would do!

Is it true that pirates really buried big wooden chests of gold coins? To find out, figure out where to put the letters in each column of this puzzle. The letters all fit in the boxes under their own columns, but not always in the same order!

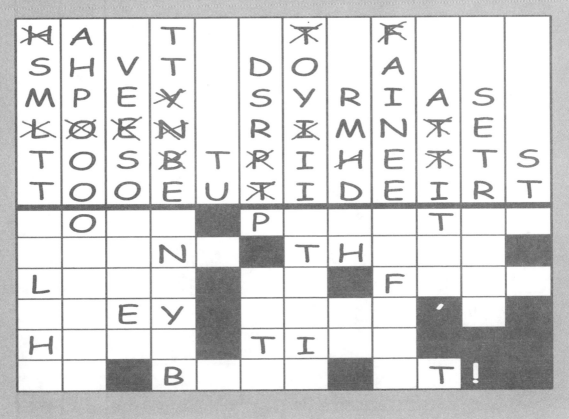

Shared Loot

Two pirates got equal shares of the loot, but they did not get exactly the same items. Look carefully at what is in their bags. Find the two pieces of jewelry that do not appear in both bags.

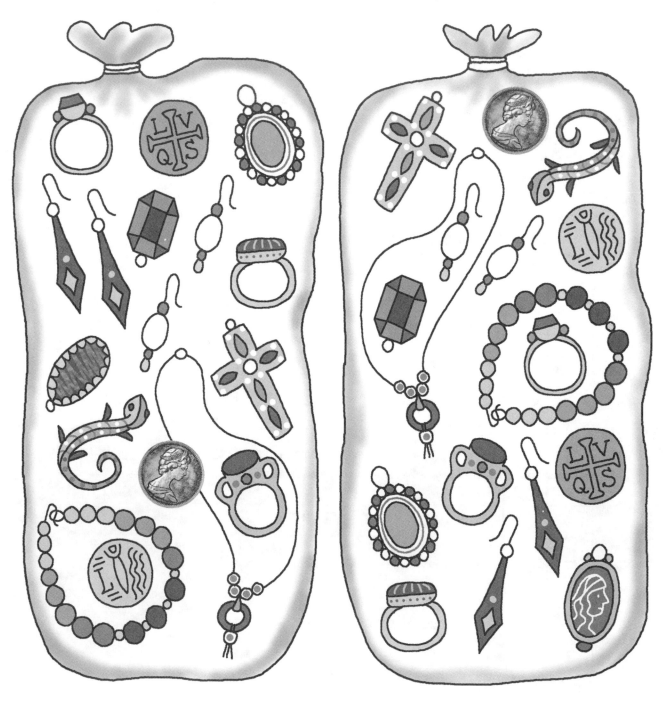

Heap O' Coins

All the pirate treasure has been dumped in this big pile. See if you can answer the following questions:

1. **How many different types of coins are there?**

2. **Which coin is seen the most?**

3. **Of which coin is there only one?**

4. **Are there more light gold coins or dark silver coins?**

A Pirate's Doubloons

Doubloons were Spanish gold coins that pirates loved to steal! Two of them next to each other look very much like double letter Os (or silly pirate eyes). Use the clues to come up with each of these OO words.

Pirate's peg-legs were made of this = _ O O _

Another word for pirate treasure = _ O O _ _

Pirates ate "salmagundy" with this = _ _ O O _

A captured pirate might hang from this = _ O O _ _

A kind of pirate ship with two masts = _ _ O O _

Bad pirate left on a deserted island = _ _ _ O O _ _ _

Pirates liked this kind of skin art = _ _ _ _ O O

Pirates saw this shine in the night sky = _ O O _

An infected cut from a cutlass might do this = O O _ _

Loud noise from a pirate's cannon = _ O O _

Sunken Treasure

Gather up the few items listed here and very shortly you will be plunking coins into your own Davy Jones's Locker.

What you need:

1 large glass jar with a lid, such as a large mayo or pickle jar

1 small plastic ship

clean sand or fish tank gravel

water

blue food coloring (optional)

coins

What to do:

First make sure the mouth of the jar is wide enough for your ship to fit through.

1. Pour about an inch of sand or gravel into the bottom of the jar.

2. Bury most of the ship in the sand.

3. Pour water into the jar until it is three quarters full.

4. If desired, add a few drops of food coloring to turn your "ocean" blue.

5. Have an adult help you make a coin slot in the lid of the jar.

6. Drop coins through the slot and enjoy your sunken treasure!

Avast!

"Davy Jones's Locker" is a sailor's term for the bottom of the ocean, especially meant as a grave for drowned sailors, lost treasure, and sunken ships. No one really knows where this term came from, but it was first used around 1750.

NOTE: To keep "stuff" from growing in the water, try adding a few tablespoons of white vinegar, or stir several tablespoons of table salt into the water before you pour it into the jar.

Where's My Share?

These four treasure chests have been divided in half. The contents of each whole chest adds up to 100. Count the treasure in each half chest and write the amount next to it. Write the letters of the two halves that go together on the lines below.

Chapter 8

Catch 'Em If You Can

To Catch a Thief

Many governments spent a lot of time and money trying to rid the seas of pirates. Can you fit all of the words that mean "to catch" into their proper place in the crisscross? We've left you some G-O-T-C-H-As to get you started.

SNARE

GRASP

CORNER

ARREST

SEIZE

STOP

CAPTURE

BAG

SNATCH

TRAP

GRAB

EXTRA FUN:

The word THIEF is hiding in the grid, too. It is only spelled correctly one time, and it is in white letters. Can you find it?

What a Way to Go

Twelve pirates have been found guilty. If all of the following statements are true, what is the correct fraction for each method of punishment?

None of the women pirates will be executed.

All of the pirates wearing hats will be hung.

Any pirate with a long braid will lose his head.

The rest of the pirates will be shot.

Hanging

Firing Squad

Beheading

Prison

Full Ahead

In the early nineteenth century, a particular invention made it much more difficult for the pirates to escape the navies that were hunting them down. Use the directions to cross words out of the grid. Read the remaining words from left to right and top to bottom to see why pirates were suddenly running scared!

Cross out all the words...
- that are also numbers
- that have two letters and start with an "A"
- that rhyme with "oar"
- that end with the letters "ck"

ONE	NAVY	AT	SHIPS
BECAME	MORE	POWERED	THREE
BY	STEAM	SHORE	AND
AN	COULD	EASILY	BACK
CATCH	TWO	SORE	PIRATE
SHIPS	TRUCK	AM	THAT
WORE	DEPENDED	ON	FIVE
THE	DOOR	THICK	WIND

Standing Room Only

The hanging of a pirate was a public spectacle. Huge crowds came to the gallows to watch the event. Can you find your way through this crowd and up to the noose?

OOPS! The pirate that was supposed to be hanged has escaped! Can you see him in the crowd?

START

END

Off with His Head!

In China, the most common punishment for a pirate was to cut off his head. Beheadings were a public event, and the more heads that rolled, the better!

Can you figure out these seven picture puzzles?
Each one shows a common compound word that starts with H-E-A-D.

What does the hangman like to read when he's not hanging pirates?

Use this decoder to find the silly answer to the riddle above.

A = ❖   O = ☆

C = ☆   P = ▲

E = ✖   R = ■

H = ⬤   S = ✪

N = ☠   T = ✺

That Hurts!

What did the pirate say when the firing squad shot him through the chest?
Color in the O-U-C-Hs. Then read the remaining white letters to find out.

OUCHOUCHARRROUCHR!OUCH
OUCHMOUCHEOUCHOUCHOUCHH
EAOUCHROUCHOUCHTOUCHY!

91

A Hunting You Will Go

It is your turn to hunt for pirates! Use a colored marker to run a line through the name of each pirate as you find it in the letter grid.

Aruj Barbarossa
Samuel Bellamy
Edward Teach
Red Beard
Captain Kidd
Bartholomew
    Roberts
Calico Jack
Jack Rackham
Khizr Barbarossa
Blackbeard
Edward England
Black Bart
Anne Bonny
Mary Read
John Avery
Edward Low
Cheng I Sao
Captain Hook

Extra Fun!

When you have caught all the pirates, read the remaining letters from left to right and top to bottom to find a pirate joke!

```
S H D D I K N I A T P A C O W B
A D A S S O R A B R A B J U R A
M A H K C A R K C A J O Y O U R
U W O L D R A W D E C A T J A T
E C E D W A R D T E A C H O S H
L H A P I R A T T E ? H H H S O
B I R D E I N R T H K E K N O L
E E E B U S A H E O S N C A R O
L A D N D B M A O K D G A V A M
L E B N K O I H S A E I J E B E
A L E C I K N E E A G S O R R W
M O A L D I D R O U B A C Y A R
Y L R L A O Y O N . W O I H B O
B E D T D R A E B K C A L B R B
N A P P A I R A T E C O A M Z E
E A S M , Y O U C A N G C R I R
C E D W A R D E N G L A N D H T
A B Y N N O B E N N A H I M ! K S
```

Keep Hunting

Look at the list of pirates you were hunting on the page to the left. See if you can complete the following hunting tasks.

1. Match three common men's names with their pirate names.

2. Find the two pirates who were brothers.

3. Find the name in the list that means the same as "Barbarossa."

4. Find the three women pirates.

5. Find the one fictional pirate in the list.

Grim Warning

After a pirate was caught and executed, his body might be displayed in a "gibbet" as a warning to other pirates. This awful contraption was a series of chains and metal straps that held the dead pirate until there was nothing left but bones! Pirates were measured for their gibbet while they were still alive. Break the "Switch The Vowel Code" to see how the pirates felt about this.

Et wus sued thut u peruta faurad baeng mausorad fir hes gebbat mira thun uctoully baeng axacotad!

Pardon Me?

Some pirates were let go, or pardoned, after being caught. Why? Figure out where to put each of the scrambled letters below. They all fit under their own columns, but not always in the same order. Black boxes stand for the spaces between words. When you have filled in the grid correctly, you will know why these men were not imprisoned or executed like the rest of their shipmates.

B		R	N		A	O	G		A	I		I	R		
B̶	E	R̶	I	M	I̶	T	D		I	I		H	T̶	D	B
A	A	E̶	O	R	F̶	E	R̶		M̶	D	G	H̶	N	T	T
B	E	P	D	O	N	N	E	C	E	F	P	I	E	A	O	E

	■						■	M				■		
P						■			■		H	'	■		
		E	■	F		R			■				■		
						■		■			R				

Easy Off?

Break the Number Substitution Code (1=A, 2=B, etc.) to read this riddle.

23-8-1-20   7-15-5-19   8-1   8-1   8-1

16-12-15-16?   1   16-9-18-1-20-5

12-1-21-7-8-9-14-7   8-9-19   8-5-1-4   15-6-6!

Sad Pirate, Glad Pirate

This pirate doesn't yet know his fate. Help the might-be-beheaded "sad pirate" move through the maze so he becomes a will-be-pardoned "glad pirate" at the end. Make a path that alternates sad and glad. You can move up and down, or side to side, but not diagonally. If you hit a "dead pirate," you are *definitely* going in the wrong direction!

START

END

Pirate Buster

Pirates were in trouble when navies started to build huge boats with lots of cannons. Fill in all the spaces below that contain two dots. You will learn the name of these giant navy boats that could defeat even the most determined pirates.

Avast!
It took more than 2,000 trees to build a "pirate buster" ship large enough to carry 100 heavy cannons.

Chapter 9

They're Still at It

Read a Pirate

Pirates are colorful characters that practically leap from the pages of a book. Even books that were written over 100 years ago are still popular today. Solve the rebus puzzles and you will know the titles of two very famous books featuring pirates. Check them out at your local library!

Avast!
The fictional Captain Hook was given many characteristics of the real Blackbeard!

P+ [feet] -F +R [pan]

[treasure] [eye] +L+ [hand] -H

These stories are also popular in another form. Break the code below to see how else you could enjoy a modern version of a good old-fashioned pirate story.

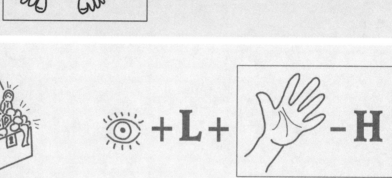

A ●   M △   I ■   S ☆

E ○   O ▲   K □   V ★

● ☆   ●   △ ▲ ★ ■ ○ [coin]

Pirate Flick

Pirate movies are full of action and adventure—that's why they are still such popular entertainment today! Can you figure out the picture code and learn which movie these kids are watching?

Computer Pirates

Not all modern pirates travel by boat. High-tech pirates travel by Internet! These cyberpirates loot billions of dollars each year by stealing software programs, music files, video games, and more. They can even break into a bank's computer system and electronically snatch huge amounts of money! What is the common name for these techno-thieves? To find out, fill in all the boxes with a 0 or 1 inside.

1	2	0	4	1	1	0	7	1	0	3	0	4	1	8	0	1	8	0	1	0	2	1	0
0	3	1	6	1	6	1	2	1	2	3	1	7	0	6	1	2	4	1	3	1	2	0	6
1	0	0	7	0	0	0	3	0	3	9	1	0	8	2	0	1	2	0	1	0	6	1	0
0	2	0	2	1	6	1	8	0	9	6	0	7	0	4	1	3	9	0	0	4	8	2	1
1	4	1	9	0	8	1	9	0	1	5	0	7	1	2	1	0	7	1	7	0	2	1	0

There are also regular people who may be a type of computer pirate without even knowing it. Crack the keyboard code to see if you are one of them!

8R   697   8HW5QOO   6974   W9R52Q43

9H   J943   5YQH   9H3   D9J*7534,   697

D97OE   G3   G43QI8HT   5Y3   OQ2!

Scary Seas

In many parts of the world, piracy is still going strong! Scattered around the page are the names of thirteen countries that still have pirate problems. Figure out where they belong in the grid. After writing in the names, read the shaded letters from top to bottom to learn where you can find the most pirates today.

BRAZIL

BORNEO

SOMALIA

REPUBLIC

JAMAICA

GHANA

PERU

INDONESIA

DOMINICAN

ECUADOR

MALAYSIA

INDIA

HAITI

BANGLADESH

Zoom Zoom

If you saw a modern pirate approaching, he would not be in a large sailing vessel. Connect the dots in order to see what his boat would more likely look like.

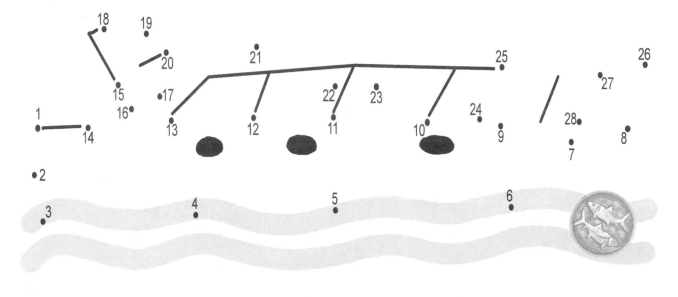

What's the Motive?

Pirates act when the chance of reward is great and the risk of getting caught is small. Today's pirates are motivated by the same thing as pirates from long ago. To find out what that is, fill in all the letters that are *not* R, D, E, or G, then read the remaining letters.

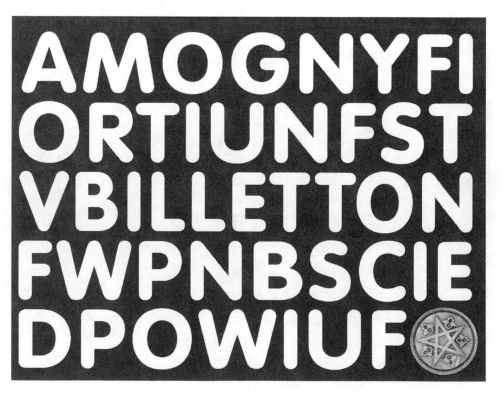

Pirate Gizmos...

Today's pirates make use of the latest technology to help find and follow the boats they plan to attack. Use the "Plan To Attack" decoder to find six of their fancy tools. Oh yeah, there's one very old-fashioned tool in the list, too. Pirates still use this to help them board a ship when they finally close in!

Awwwk! Where's the cargo? Where's the cargo?

P	L	A	N		T	O		A	T	T	A	C	K
1	2	3	4		5	6						7	8

S 1 E E D B 6 3 5

7 E 2 2   1 H 6 4 E

R 3 D 3 R

C 6 M 1 U 5 E R

R 3 D I 6   S 7 3 4 4 E R

5 R 3 7 8 I 4 G   D E V I 7 E

G R 3 1 1 2 I 4 G   I R 6 4

...vs. Anti-Pirate Gadgets

Today's sailors have found a clever way of using technology to keep modern pirates on their own boat! Break the "Sounds Like" Code to learn how.

Thay uh aht ach eh Lake tree ka phense tood a ray ling "Arrrr" ownda thuh bow ta. Zeh ah pa!

Look Around

Step one in protecting against modern pirate attacks is to know where the pirates are. Merchant shipowners can purchase Unmanned Aerial Vehicles to fly a patrol around their boats looking for unusual activity. This UAV is flying a little too close to things. What items do you think it has spotted? Are there any pirates among them?

Hit and Run

Many modern pirates like to steal small things so they can move quickly. There are ten of these items hiding in the grid below. Add the missing letter to the one item hiding in each line. Use all the extra letters.

C A M E C A S	R A S J E W E
L R Y D J E W	L R Y R U G S
C I G A R D R	G S E T T E S
C R E C I G A	E T T E S D I
T C A C R E D	T C A R D S R
D S T E L C O	P U T E R S E
V T E L E V I	I O N S I S I
O N S C A S V	R S H J E W E
L R Y D R U S	V D S G S C A
M E R A S A C	M E R A S S H

H C R
I D S
U A E M

EXTRA FUN:
How many of these items would interest old-fashioned pirates, too?

Got Cargo?

While some pirates steal just a few valuable items, other pirates take the whole boat, its crew, and all of its cargo! There is a special term for this type of piracy. Figure out what letters are missing from each column of words. The same set of letters is missing for all words in a column. Then put the four letter sections together to spell the answer.

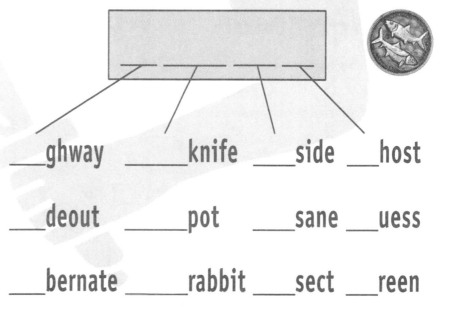

___ghway   ____knife   ___side   __host

___deout   ____pot   ___sane   __uess

___bernate   ____rabbit   ___sect   __reen

105

Low Tech

Sometimes the best way to fight modern pirates is with old-fashioned cleverness! What are these sailors using to convince the pirate to stay on his own boat? First connect the numbered dots in order. Then use a single straight line to connect each letter pair.

High Tech

There are all kinds of new inventions to give merchant ship captains an early warning that pirates might be planning an attack. To see a list of some of them, fill in the one letter that is missing from each line. Then figure out which letter the watchful "eye" represents.

ADA and _AD👁OS

SE_UR👁TY _AMERAS

_L_CTR👁C F_NC_S

_OW-_👁GHT B👁NOCU_ARS

_M_RG_NCY S👁R_NS

M_T👁_N SENS_RS

F_OOD_👁GHTS

👁NT_UDE_ ALA_MS

Old or New?

Modern pirates still act a lot like old-fashioned pirates, even if they do look slightly different. Can you find eight clues that tell you which of these pirates is still lurking on the high seas today?

ARRR!

Avast!
The French word for someone who hijacks an airplane is "pirate de l'air."

Today's Treasure Hunt

You've reached the end of the book, but we have one final puzzle for you. Hidden throughout the book are these four coins...

This coin is worth $.25

This coin is worth $.50

This coin is worth $1.00

This coin is worth $5.00

Grab a separate piece of paper to use as a tally sheet. Now look at every page—including the introduction—and count how many of each kind of coin you find in the whole book. Not every page has a coin, and some pages have more than one, so look sharp! Write the total number of each coin you find under its picture. HINT: The four coins on this page don't count!

Now, answer these questions!

> ## How much is the total treasure of coins worth?

> ## If you divide the booty evenly with your three best mates, how much will you each get?

ARRR! This be me favoritest kind o' puzzle!

Look Again!

Just when you be thinkin' that all the pirates had sailed fer home port, they be back! Use yer eagle eye to spot each of these picture pieces somewhere in this here book. Write the name of the puzzle each piece be from in the space under each box. Avast! There be only one picture piece from each chapter!

1.

2.

3.

4.

5.

6.

7.

8.

9.

Appendix 2
References

If you can't get enough of pirates, here are some books and films you might want to check out at your local library, bookstore, or movie store.

Books

AMAZING WORLD OF PIRATES, by Philip Steele (2003)

Loaded with information about piracy from ancient times to the present. Includes pirate craft projects to try as well.

PIRATE, by Richard Platt (2004)

An Eyewitness Book filled with stunning photographs of pirate artifacts. Ideal for nonfiction browsing!

PIRATES PAST NOON, by Mary Pope Osborne (1994)

One of the Magic Tree House series where Jack and Annie are whisked back to the time of pirates. Also look for the nonfiction companion book: PIRATES (2001).

PETER PAN, by J. M. Barrie (1904)

The literary classic about Peter Pan, the boy who would not grow up. Fly with him and the Darling children to Neverland and meet the infamous Captain Hook.

PETER & THE STARCATCHERS, by Dave Barry and Ridley Pearson (2004)

A silly, fast-paced prequel (of sorts) to the classic Peter Pan book. See how Peter came to fly and join him on all sorts of high-seas adventures.

TREASURE ISLAND (1883), by Robert Louis Stevenson

The most famous pirate adventure of all times! Young Jim Hawkins is caught up in the search for buried treasure with the pirate Long John Silver.

EVERYTHING I KNOW ABOUT PIRATES (2000), by Tom Lichtenheld

"A collection of made-up facts, educated guesses, and silly pictures about the bad guys of the high seas." This is the author's own description of his book!

Films

PETER PAN (1953)

There have been several films of this classic story, but the Disney version is our favorite.

HOOK (1991)

Steven Spielberg's remake of the Peter Pan story where Peter is all grown up and must return to Neverland to save his children who have been kidnapped by Captain Hook.

PIRATES OF THE CARIBBEAN: THE CURSE OF THE BLACK PEARL (2003)

Will Turner must team up with the pirate Jack Sparrow to save the woman he loves and help break the nasty curse that plagues the pirate crew. Look for the sequel, **PIRATES OF THE CARIBBEAN: DEAD MAN'S CHEST**, in 2006.

TREASURE ISLAND (1950)

One of several film versions of the classic book listed above.

PIRATES OF PENZANCE (1983)

Movie adaptation of the Gilbert and Sullivan comic operetta where a young man is mistakenly apprenticed to a pirate.

CAPTAIN BLOOD (1935)

A pirate adventure done in the grand Hollywood style. This was one of the first movies to change the pirate character from a scurvy dog to a romantic action hero. Starring Errol Flynn, Olivia de Havilland, and Basil Rathbone, this movie is a classic! If you like CAPTAIN BLOOD, you'll want to see THE SEA HAWK (1940), also starring Errol Flynn.

Web Sites

www.dltk-kids.com/crafts/pirates/pirates.html

DLTK's Crafts for Kids features a variety of fun, printable children's crafts, coloring pages, and more. The site is run by a mom with her two girls as official craft testers and the dad as technical support. Suitable for younger pirates!

www.thepiratesrealm.com/index.shtml

A great all-purpose pirate site, packed with information both historical and hysterical! Learn about boats, weapons, customs, famous pirates, and modern pirate festivals. Lots of pictures, lots of info, lots of fun. Better for older pirates!

www.nationalgeographic.com/pirates

This site features links to other safe National Geographic pirate "ports" for the history of famous pirates and pirate life, an extensive reading list, and an online game called "High Seas Adventure," which has three separate mystery story lines to follow and solve. Good for pirates of all ages!

Puzzle Answers

page vi • Ahoy, Me Hearties!

1C T	2A O		3A G	4D E	5D T		6F T	7G O
8G T	9C H	10E E		11E S	12F E	13G C	14E O	15B N	16A D-
17F H	18F A	19D N	20E D		21C S	22B T	23C O	24C R	25B E!

A. Barking pet
$$\underset{16}{D} \ \underset{2}{O} \ \underset{3}{G}$$

B. After nine
$$\underset{22}{T} \ \underset{25}{E} \ \underset{15}{N}$$

C. Not tall
$$\underset{21}{S} \ \underset{9}{H} \ \underset{23}{O} \ \underset{24}{R} \ \underset{1}{T}$$

D. Fish catcher
$$\underset{19}{N} \ \underset{4}{E} \ \underset{5}{T}$$

E. How much medicine to take at one time
$$\underset{20}{D} \ \underset{14}{O} \ \underset{11}{S} \ \underset{10}{E}$$

F. Dislike very much
$$\underset{17}{H} \ \underset{18}{A} \ \underset{6}{T} \ \underset{12}{E}$$

G. Camping bed
$$\underset{13}{C} \ \underset{7}{O} \ \underset{8}{T}$$

page 2 • Turkish Delight?

ARRRR! A nice, fat hostage such as yourself should bring

X + V + I + I + I + I + I

20

pieces of gold!

Are you nuts?! I'm worth at least

C - L - X + V + V

50

pieces of gold!

page 3 • Funny Guy

What pirate was known for his practical jokes?

C	B	G	A	G	B
H	F	M	J	H	M
P	J	T	H	J	A
G	M	J	B	F	H
F	I	H	M	N	F
J	H	M	J	M	J
K	J	I	B	H	D
M	G	J	G	B	G
F	D	M	B	M	H
M	-	E	J	R	G
B	H	J	F	M	G

CAPTAIN KIDD-ER

ARRRR! That's NOT funny!

page 4 • Buccaneers

page 4 • Privateers

Letter 'tween D & F = E
Letter after T = U
Letter always with U = Q
Letter 'fore S = R
First letter = A
Letter 'tween L & N = M
Sixth letter = F
Three letters 'fore R = O
Letter 'tween Q & S = R
One letter after D = E
Letter after S = T
Letter 'fore U = T
Fifth letter = E
Letter 'tween K & M = L

112

Puzzle Answers

page 5 • Queen's Favorite

HE WAS MADE A KNIGHT

page 7 • Special Effects

Blackbeard stuck pieces of burning, smoking rope under the edge of his hat!

Everyone will draw a different picture. Here's ours!

page 6 • Ready or Not, Here We Come!

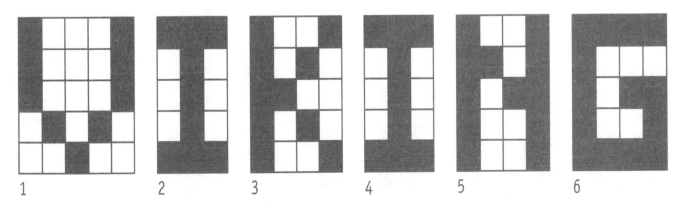

1   2   3   4   5   6

page 8 and 9 • The Barbarossa Brothers

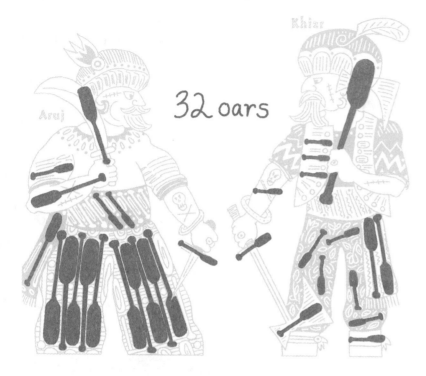

32 oars

page 10 • A Particular Pirate

CRIMSON WAISTCOAT

CRIMSON BRITCHES

THREE CORNERED HAT

RED FEATHER

SILK SASH

WITH PISTOLS

DIAMOND CROSS

GOLD CHAIN

page 8 • Barbarossa Nickname

RED BEARD

page 9 • Which Brother

Aruj the elder brother. Khizr, the younger, had a beard that was brown!

page 9 • First Job

1. PIRATE
2. PIATER
3. POATER
4. POTTER

page 9 • Honor Memory

He dyed his beard and moustache red with henna!

page 11 • **All in the Family**

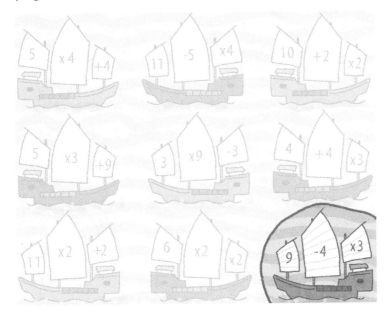

page 12 • **Pirate Queens**

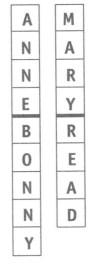

| A |
| N |
| N |
| E |
| B |
| O |
| N |
| N |
| Y |

| M |
| A |
| R |
| Y |
| R |
| E |
| A |
| D |

CALICO

JACK

page 16 • **Sounds Like . . .**

1. The sides and bottom of a boat = H U L L *(NOT SHINY)* → DULL
2. The floor of a ship = D E C K *(QUICK KISS)*
3. Tall pole that supports the sails = M A S T *(NOT SLOW)*
4. The left side of the ship P O R T *(PLACE TO PLAY TENNIS)*
5. Space to store the ship's cargo = H O L D *(NOT HOT)*
7. Heavy piece of metal that keeps ship in place = A N C H O R *(ONE WHO COUNTS MONEY)*
8. Sheet of canvas used to catch the wind = S A I L *(BUCKET)*
9. Ropes that control sails = R I G G I N G *(MAKING A HOLE IN DIRT)*
10. Piece of wood or metal used to steer the ship = R U D D E R *(WHERE A COW MAKES MILK)*
12. Small, round window in the side of a boat = P O R T H O L E *(WHERE SANTA LIVES)*

BONUS: Small lookout platform high on a mast = C R O W ' S   N E S T *(ENEMY'S EXAM)*

page 14 • **Frightful Flag**

Puzzle Answers

page 17 • **Nasty Knots**

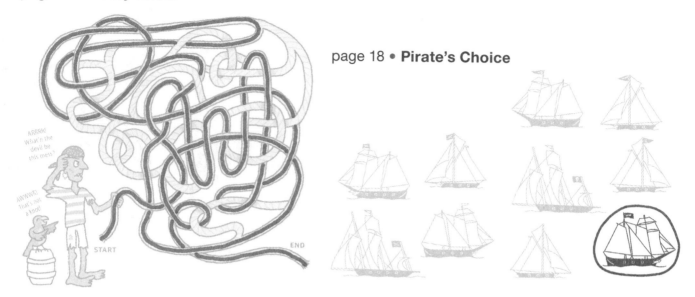

page 18 • **Pirate's Choice**

page 20 • **Sails in the Wind**

page 21 • **Fierce Figurehead**

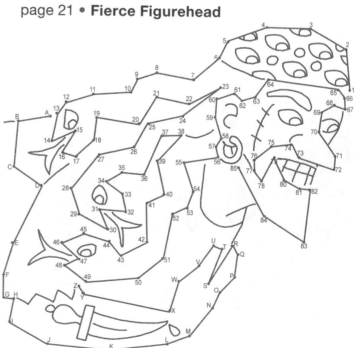

page 22 • Going Up

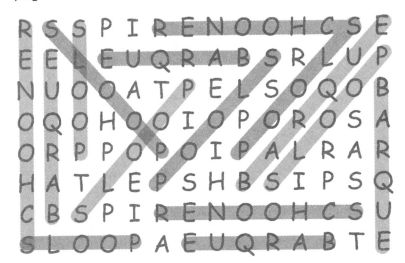

page 23 • Black Jacks

Boat floor inspection = D E C K   C H E C K

Freezing cargo space = C O L D   H O L D

Weak sheet of canvas = F R A I L   S A I L

Not shiny bottom of boat = D U L L   H U L L

Wonderful fellow pirate = G R E A T   M A T E

Cleanser for strong cords = R O A P   S O A P

Bonus: Final sail-supporting pole explosion =
L A S T   M A S T   B L A S T

page 23 • Sneaky

page 22 • Going Down

1. F A S T E N
2. S E C U R E
3. A T T A C H

Puzzle Answers

page 24 • **When is the best time . . .**

When is the best time to buy a pirate ship?

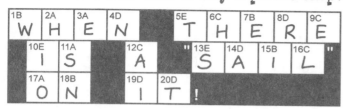

1B W	2A H	3A E	4D N		5E T	6C H	7B E	8D R	9C E
	10E I	11A S		12C A	"13E S	14D A	15B I	16C L	"
	17A O	18B N		19D I	20D T	!			

A. Foot covering
$\underline{S}\ \underline{H}\ \underline{O}\ \underline{E}$
11 2 17 3

B. Grape drink
$\underline{W}\ \underline{I}\ \underline{N}\ \underline{E}$
1 15 18 7

C. To cure
$\underline{H}\ \underline{E}\ \underline{A}\ \underline{L}$
6 9 12 16

D. Choo-choo
$\underline{T}\ \underline{R}\ \underline{A}\ \underline{I}\ \underline{N}$
20 8 14 19 4

E. Command to a dog
$\underline{S}\ \underline{I}\ \underline{T}$
13 10 5

page 26 • **Pirate Talk**

page 27 • **Is He a Pirate?**

A pirate...

...who wears an eyepatch can only **W I N K**.

...is fierce; he wears black, not **P I N K**.

...doesn't take baths, so he will **S T I N K**.

...isn't a nice guy; he's a rotten **F I N K**.

...hates milk; he wants rum to **D R I N K**.

...has gold coins that jingle and **C L I N K**.

...who is stupid doesn't **T H I N K**

   his ship will **S I N K**.

page 28 • **Double Trouble**

Puzzle Answers

page 29 • How could the poor pirate . . . ?

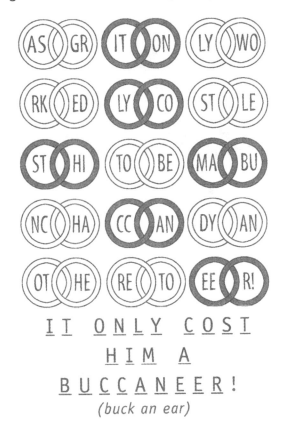

(AS⟩⟨GR) (IT⟩⟨ON) (LY⟩⟨WO)

(RK⟩⟨ED) (LY⟩⟨CO) (ST⟩⟨LE)

(ST⟩⟨HI) (TO⟩⟨BE) (MA⟩⟨BU)

(NC⟩⟨HA) (CC⟩⟨AN) (DY⟩⟨AN)

(OT⟩⟨HE) (RE⟩⟨TO) (EE⟩⟨R!)

IT ONLY COST

HIM A

BUCCANEER!

(buck an ear)

page 31 • Hairs to You!

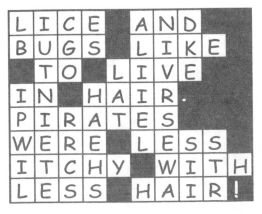

L	I	C	E		A	N	D
B	U	G	S		L	I	K	E
		T	O		L	I	V	E
I	N		H	A	I	R	.
P	I	R	A	T	E	S
W	E	R	E		L	E	S	S
I	T	C	H	Y		W	I	T	H
L	E	S	S		H	A	I	R	!

page 30 • What ARRRR Pirates Like?

In what do pirate captains sit?
ARRRRm chairs!

What kind of socks do pirates like best?
ARRRRgyles!

Where do pirates never go?
ARRRRt museums!

What do pirates do when they disagree?
ARRRRgue!

What is a pirate's favorite sport?
ARRRRchery!

page 33 • Perfect Pirate Pets

1. CAT   2. MONKEY   3. PARROT   4. RAT

Puzzle Answers

page 34 • **Filthy Stinkin' Pirates**

~~AT~~	(IT)	~~BOOT~~	(WAS)	~~FLIP-FLOP~~
(EASIER)	~~SOAPED~~	(TO)	~~SQUIRT~~	(STEAL)
~~SKIRT~~	(CLEAN)	~~CLOG~~	(CLOTHES)	~~SCRUBBED~~
(THAN)	~~AM~~	(WASH)	~~SANDAL~~	~~AN~~
~~RINSED~~	(DIRTY)	~~SHIRT~~	(CLOTHES)	~~SLIPPER~~

page 35 • **Whose Boots?**

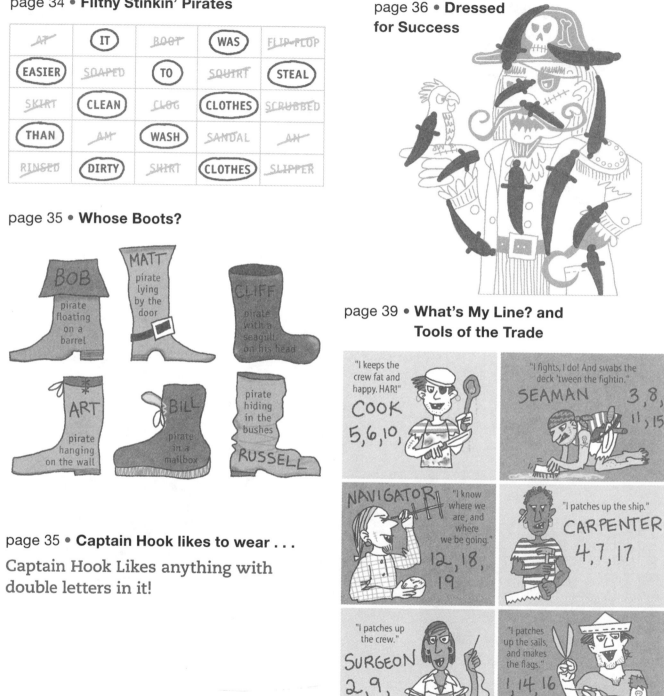

BOB — pirate floating on a barrel

MATT — pirate lying by the door

CLIFF — pirate with a seagull on his head

ART — pirate hanging on the wall

BILL — pirate in a mailbox

RUSSELL — pirate hiding in the bushes

page 35 • **Captain Hook likes to wear . . .**

Captain Hook Likes anything with double letters in it!

page 36 • **Dressed for Success**

page 39 • **What's My Line? and Tools of the Trade**

"I keeps the crew fat and happy. HAR!"
COOK 5, 6, 10,

"I fights, I do! And swabs the deck 'tween the fightin."
SEAMAN 3, 8, 11, 15

NAVIGATOR "I know where we are, and where we be going." 12, 18, 19

"I patches up the ship."
CARPENTER 4, 7, 17

"I patches up the crew."
SURGEON 2, 9, 13, 20

"I patches up the sails, and makes the flags." 1, 14, 16
SAILMAKER

Puzzle Answers

page 40 • Crowded Cargo

page 42 • Sea Legs

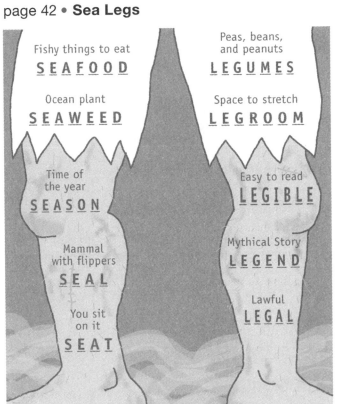

Fishy things to eat
SEAFOOD

Ocean plant
SEAWEED

Time of the year
SEASON

Mammal with flippers
SEAL

You sit on it
SEAT

Peas, beans, and peanuts
LEGUMES

Space to stretch
LEGROOM

Easy to read
LEGIBLE

Mythical Story
LEGEND

Lawful
LEGAL

page 41 • Awww, Cap'n, Do I Have To?

SCRUB	DECKS
PUMP	BILGES
CATCH	RATS
SCRAPE	HULL
SIFT	GUNPOWDER
SHINE	CANNONBALLS
PLUG	LEAKS
RETIE	KNOTS
PULL	TEETH

page 41 • Sea Sick

Pirate cooks must work hard to make tender meat. (2, 10)

If our weight is even, the boat won't sink quickly. (4, 8, 7)

As evening approaches, the south reef comes into view. (7, 3)

If I've got an inexpert sailor, it won't be smooth sailing. (5, 9, 2)

After the sixth storm, most of our teeny sails were gone. (6, 14, 1)

The pirates have been waiting 78 days for treasure!

page 43 • Yuck!

Slice leather knapsack into thin pieces and soak. Beat between stones to make tender. Scrape off the hair, then roast. Cut into smaller pieces and serve with lots of water.

page 44 • Scrub-a-Dub-Dub

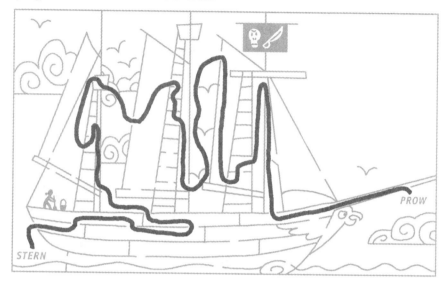

page 43 • Yum!

SHIF = F I S H

BRAC = C R A B

RAGCLI = G A R L I C

TEAM = M E A T

GABBACE = C A B B A G E

GRINEVA = V I N E G A R

TRUIF = F R U I T

OONIN = O N I O N

RAHD-LOIBED SEGG = H A R D - B O I L E D E G G S

SCIPES = S P I C E S

Pirate stew is "SALMAGUNDI"

page 44 • What's so Funny?

Cross out all the times the pirates say "YO HO."

~~YO HO~~W HY~~YO HO~~ COULD ~~YO HO~~N'T
~~YO HO~~ THE~~YO HO~~PIR ATE
~~YO HO~~ PLA Y~~YO HO~~CA RDS?
~~YO HO~~BEC AUSE~~YO HO~~H
E~~YO HO~~ WAS~~YO HO~~S ITTIN
G~~YO HO~~ ON ~~YO HO~~
THE~~YO HO~~DEC K~~YO HO~~!

Puzzle Answers

page 45 • Silly Sentences

<u>C</u>razy <u>C</u>ooks <u>C</u>hop <u>C</u>arrots.
<u>S</u>ails <u>S</u>lap <u>S</u>even <u>S</u>illy <u>S</u>eagulls.
<u>W</u>ild <u>W</u>ind <u>W</u>hips <u>W</u>et <u>W</u>hitecaps.
<u>P</u>irates <u>P</u>ractice <u>P</u>lundering.
<u>R</u>ats <u>R</u>ehearse <u>R</u>igging <u>R</u>aces.
<u>F</u>rightening <u>F</u>lags <u>F</u>lap <u>F</u>itfully.

page 45 • Watch Out!

7 bells — MIDNIGHT
5 bells — 12:30 AM
2 bells — 1:00 AM
3 bells — 1:30 AM
6 bells — 2:00 AM
4 bells — 2:30 AM
3:00 AM
3:30 AM
4:00 AM

page 47 • Knot Right!

K N T O K O T K
N O N K N K T T
T T K O T O K O
O O O T N K N K
O N K K T O O N
K N O K N T O T
K O N T T N K O
N K O N O K N O

page 51 • Codes of Conduct

Rule 1:
(reverse alphabet)
OBEY THE CAPTAIN.

Rule 2:
(alphabet shift)
NO FIGHTING
BETWEEN PIRATES.

Rule 3:
(reverse number subst.)
NO WOMEN
ON BOARD.

Rule 4:
(number substitution)
NO GAMBLING
ON BOARD.

Rule 5:
(alphabet shift)
NO SLEEPING
WHEN ON DUTY.

Rule 6:
(reverse alphabet)
NO STEALING FROM
FELLOW PIRATES.

Rule 7:
(number substitution)
KEEP
WEAPONS
CLEAN
AND
READY.

BEWARE! Break the rules and pay the price!

page 48 • Sing As You Work

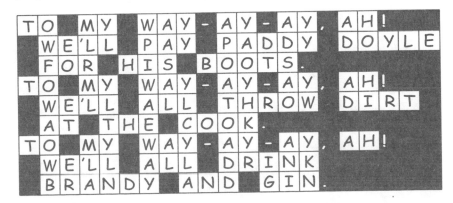

TO	MY	WAY	-AY	-AY,	AH!
WE'LL	PAY	PADDY		DOYLE
FOR	HIS	BOOTS.	
TO	MY	WAY	-AY	-AY,	AH!
WE'LL	ALL	THROW	DIRT
AT	THE	COOK.
TO	MY	WAY	-AY	-AY,	AH!
WE'LL	ALL	DRINK
BRANDY	AND	GIN.

123

Puzzle Answers

page 53 • **Mutiny!**

page 54 • **The Ultimate "Time Out"**

page 55 •
Poor Pirate!

		1D O	2E H		3F N	4D O		!
5A I		6B T	7C H	8B I	9C N	10B K		
11E I	12A '	13B V	E		14F B	15E E	16F E	17D N
18A M	19F A	20C R	21A O	22C O	23D N	24A E	25E D	!

A. What you see at a cinema
M O V I E
18 21 12 5 24

B. Toy that flies in the wind
K I T E
10 8 6 13

C. Brass musical instrument
H O R N
7 22 20 9

D. Midday
N O O N
17 1 4 23

E. To put out of sight
H I D E
2 11 25 15

F. Lima, string, or kidney
B E A N
14 16 19 3

page 56 •
Walk the Plank

PLANK
BLANK
BLINK
BRINK
DRINK

page 56 • **Ouch**

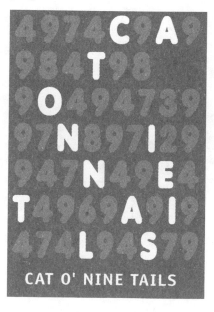

CAT O' NINE TAILS

page 57 • Double Ouch

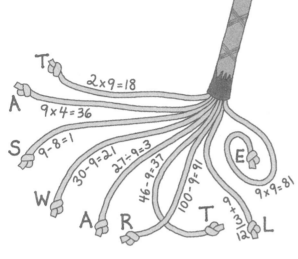

T
A $2 \times 9 = 18$
S $9 \times 4 = 36$
W $9 - 8 = 1$
    $30 - 9 = 21$
    $27 \div 9 = 3$
A $46 - 9 = 37$
R $100 - 9 = 91$
T $9 + 3 = 12$
E $9 \times 9 = 81$
L

S A L T   W A T E R

page 58 • Hanging Around

WHAT DO YOU GET IF YOU'RE CAUGHT HANGING FROM THE YARDARM? VERY SORE ARMS!

page 59 • You Better Behave!

The __Keel__ is the backbone of the boat.

Your hands would be tied with __ropE__.

Your __lEgs__ might be tied, too, so you can't swim.

The __Line__ of rope is passed underneath the boat.

Your __clotHes__ would be taken away.

You would be tossed __overboArd__.

You would sink completely __Underwater__.

You would be __pulLed__ under the boat.

And then out the other __sIde__.

Your body would scrape against sharp __barNacles__.

Hold breath in your __lunGs__ so you don't drown!

K
E
E
L
H
A
U
L
I
N
G

page 60 • Brig Breakout

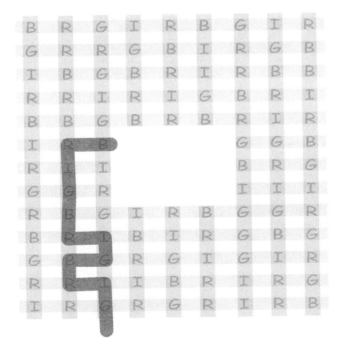

Puzzle Answers

page 62 • Boarding Party

page 64 • Junk Jam

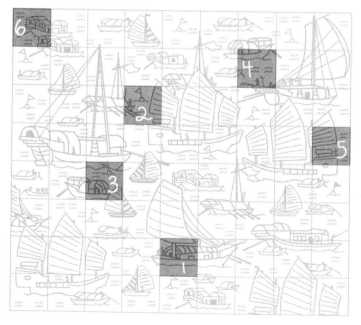

page 65 • Treacherous Trick

Possible answers:

<u>6-letter words:</u> create, search, archer, eraser, chorus, hoarse, hearse

<u>7-letter words:</u> creator, teacher, cheater, shouter, charter, reaches

page 66 • Hide and Seek

The Spanish <u>fleet</u> had nowhere
group of boats

to <u>flee</u>. They were taken control of
run away

by the Buccaneers shortly after they passed

the <u>reef</u>. The pirates <u>reeked</u>
ridge of coral   _smelled badly_

and <u>sneered</u>, showing rotten
made a nasty facial expression

<u>teeth</u>. They took the treasure,
bony mouth parts

then <u>cheered</u> their
shouted with happiness

<u>sweet</u> <u>success</u>!
not bitter   _accomplishment_

**page 67 •
What POW-er!**

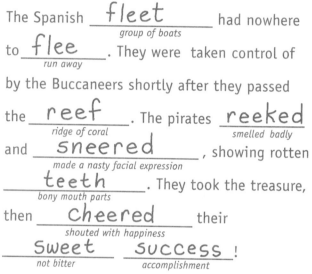

In a flash!

page 67 • Lazy Ammo

Read counter-clockwise around the circle to find the answer: "It just looks round!"

Puzzle Answers

page 68 • **Silly Sentences**

Ponytailed pirates plot poisonous parties.

Seven sloops slide silently southward.

Crashing cannonballs cut circular craters.

Dirty Dan draws dangerous daggers.

Always avoid absolutely awful ambushes!

page 68 • **I Spy**

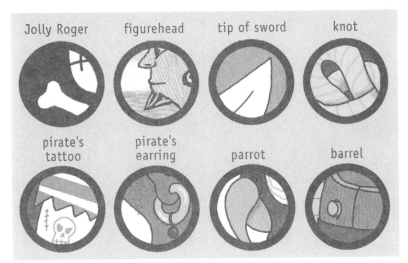

Jolly Roger · figurehead · tip of sword · knot · pirate's tattoo · pirate's earring · parrot · barrel

page 69 • **Sneaky Ship**

page 70 • **Be Afraid**

SCARE

ALARM

PANIC

SHOCK

page 70 • **Scared Ya!**

V vdavncveavrouvnd
A yaelalavioalenatlya
P pwapvepspwoprdps
O roudoegoesotuoroes
R srtramprfrerertt
I iscirieaimiloiudily
N fninrnepnistnolsn
G gmagkgegfagcegsg

page 71 • **Get a Grip**

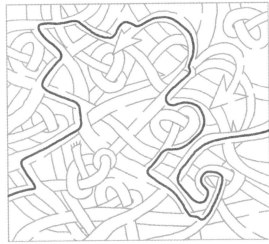

Puzzle Answers

page 72 • **Direct Hit**

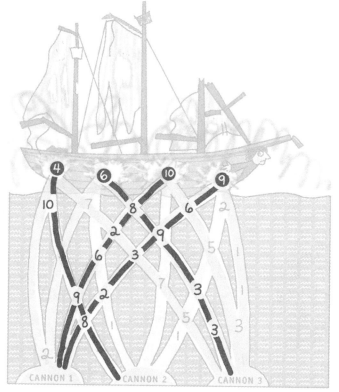

page 75 • **What to Take?**

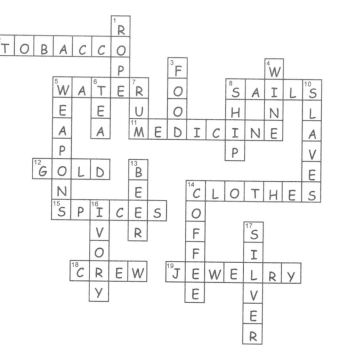

page 74 • **Whose Treasure?**

Sir Henry Morgan

Captain Kidd

Jean Laffite

Anne Bonny

Calico Jack

Black Bart

page 76 • **Hidden Treasure**

E T R E S R E T R A E S U T
E R T R E T E U T A U T R R
T E T E R U T R A E S T E E
R A R S T R R R U T R U T S
E S E T R E E S S R T R U
A R U S T A A E T U A A E R
S E R T R A S S U R E E S E
U T E E R S U E R T T E R S
R R T T U E R R E E U R E T

Puzzle Answers

page 77 • Captain Crafty's Secret Stash

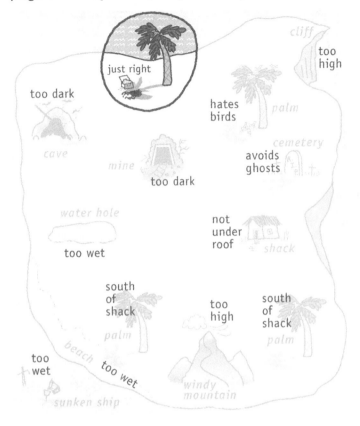

page 78 • Booty-ful!

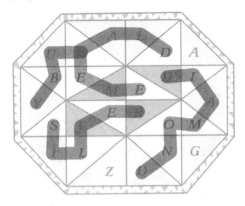

page 78 • Fill 'er Up!

If you have really stared intently, you will see what is called an "after image." This is a bright orange glowing image, and it will look like a big, shining jewel is in the middle of the treasure chest!

page 80 • Shared Loot

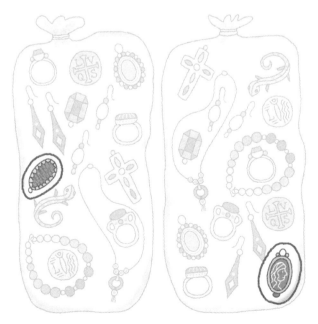

page 79 • Real Treasure?

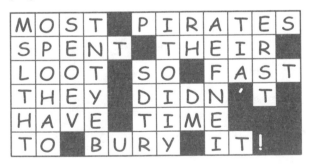

M	O	S	T		P	I	R	A	T	E	S
S	P	E	N	T		T	H	E	I	R	
L	O	O	T		S	O		F	A	S	T
T	H	E	Y		D	I	D	N	'	T	
H	A	V	E		T	I	M	E			
T	O		B	U	R	Y		I	T	!	

Puzzle Answers

page 81 • Heap O' Coins

There are the most of this coin.

These are the seven types of coins in the puzzle.

There is only one of this coin!

There are 28 gold coins and only 26 silver coins.

page 82 • A Pirate's Doubloons

Pirate's peg-legs were made of this = W O O D

Another word for pirate treasure = B O O T Y

Pirates ate "salmagundy" with this = S P O O N

A captured pirate might hang from this = N O O S E

A kind of pirate ship with two masts = S L O O P

Bad pirate left on a deserted island = M A R O O N E D

Pirates liked this kind of skin art = T A T T O O

Pirates saw this shine in the night sky = M O O N

An infected cut from a cutlass might do this = O O Z E

Loud noise from a pirate's cannon = B O O M

page 84 • Where's My Share?

page 86 • To Catch a Thief

page 87 • **What a Way to Go**

Hanging = 4/12 or 1/3

Firing Squad= 3/12 or 1/4

Beheading = 3/12 or 1/4

Prison = 2/12 or 1/6

page 88 • **Full Ahead**

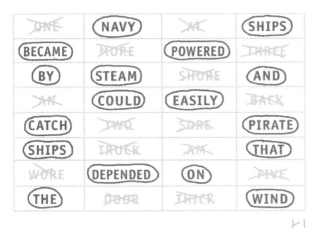

~~ONE~~	(NAVY)	~~A~~	(SHIPS)
(BECAME)	~~MORE~~	(POWERED)	~~THREE~~
(BY)	(STEAM)	~~SHORE~~	(AND)
~~AN~~	(COULD)	(EASILY)	~~BACK~~
(CATCH)	~~TWO~~	~~SORE~~	(PIRATE)
(SHIPS)	~~TRUCK~~	~~AM~~	(THAT)
~~WORE~~	(DEPENDED)	(ON)	~~FIVE~~
(THE)	~~DOOR~~	~~LATER~~	(WIND)

page 89 • **Standing Room Only**

page 90 • **Off with His Head!**

HEADACHE

HEADPHONE

HEADDRESS

HEADSTRONG

HEADQUARTERS

HEADLIGHT

HEADLINES

page 91 • **What does the hangman like to read . . .**

THE NOOSE-PAPER

Puzzle Answers

page 91 • **That Hurts!**

page 92 • **A Hunting You Will Go**

```
S H D D I K N I A T P A C O W B
A D A S S O R A B R A B J U R A
M A H K C A R K C A J O Y O U R
U W O L D R A W D E C A T J A T
E C E D W A R D T E A C H O S H
L H A P I R A T T E ? H H H S O
B I R D E I N R T H K E K N O L
E E E B U S A H E O S N C A R O
L A D N D B M A O K D G A V A M
L E B N K O I H S A E I J E B E
A L E C I K N E E A G S O R R W
M O A L D I D R O U B A C Y A R
Y L R L A O Y O N . W O I H B O
B E D T D R A E B K C A L B R B
N A P P A I R A T E C O A M Z E
E A S M , Y O U C A N G C R I R
C E D W A R D E N G L A N D H T
A B Y N N O B E N N A H I M! K S
```

Extra letters read: How do you catch a pirate? Hide in the bushes and make noise like a gold doubloon. When a pirate comes, you can grab him!

page 93 • **Keep Hunting**

1. Edward Teach was "Black-beard," Bartholomew Roberts was "Black Bart," and Jack Rackham was "Calico Jack."
2. Aruj and Khizr Barbarossa were brothers.
3. "Red Beard" means the same as "Barbarossa."
4. Mary Read, Anne Bonny, and Cheng I Sao were the three women pirates.
5. Captain Hook is the one fictional pirate in the list.

page 93 • **Grim Warning**

It was said that a pirate feared being measured for his gibbet more than actually being executed!

page 94 • Pardon Me?

A		P	I	R	A	T	E		M	I	G	H	T		B	E
P	A	R	D	O	N	E	D		I	F		H	E	'	D	
B	E	E	N		F	O	R	C	E	D		I	N	T	O	
B	E	C	O	M	I	N	G		A		P	I	R	A	T	E

page 96 • Pirate Buster

page 94 • Easy Off?

23-8-1-20   7-15-5-19   8-1   8-1   8-1
W H A T   G O E S   H A   H A   H A

16-12-15-16?   1   16-9-18-1-20-5
P L O P?   A   P I R A T E

12-1-21-7-8-9-14-7   8-9-19   8-5-1-4   15-6-6!
L A U G H I N G   H I S   H E A D   O F F!

page 95 • Sad Pirate, Glad Pirate

page 98 • Read a Pirate

P + 🦶 - F + R
PETER

🍳
PAN

💎
TREASURE

👁 + L + ✋ - H
ISLAND

⬮ ☆ ⬮ △ ▲ ★ ■ ⬭
A S   A   M O V I E

Puzzle Answers

page 99 • **Pirate Flick**

To break the code, hold the page up to a mirror. Don't read the words around the edges.

page 100 • **Computer Pirates**

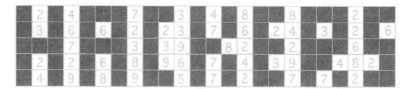

To find the correct letters look one row down, and slightly to the right, of each key listed in the code.

```
8R   697   8HW5QOO   6974   W9R52Q43
IF   YOU   INSTALL   YOUR   SOFTWARE

9H   J943   5YQH   9H3   D9J*7534,   697
ON   MORE   THAN   ONE   COMPUTER,   YOU

          D97OE   G3   G43QI8HT   5Y3   OQ2!
COULD   BE   BREAKING   THE   LAW!
```

page 101 • **Scary Seas**

SOUTH CHINA SEA

page 102 • **Zoom Zoom**

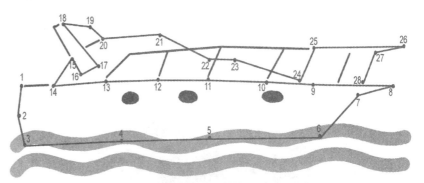

page 102 • **What's the Motive?**

Puzzle Answers

page 103 • Pirate Gizmos . . .

S P E E D B O A T
C E L L   P H O N E
R A D A R
C O M P U T E R
R A D I O   S C A N N E R
T R A C K I N G   D E V I C E
G R A P P L I N G   I R O N

page 103 • . . . vs. Anti-Pirate Gadgets

They attach electric fence to the railing around the boat. Zap!

page 104 • Look Around

PIRATE FLAG

LIGHTHOUSE

SEAGULL/BUOY

SHARK

JELLYFISH

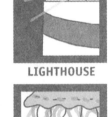

PIRATE GRAPPLING IRON

COCONUT PALM

PIRATE BOAT

SEA TURTLE

page 105 • Hit and Run

C A M E C A S H R A S J E W E
L R Y D J E W E L R Y R U G S
C I G A R D R U G S E T T E S
C R E C I G A R E T T E S D I
T C A C R E D I T C A R D S R
D S T E L C O M P U T E R S E
V T E L E V I S I O N S I S I
O N S C A S V C R S H J E W E
L R Y D R U S D V D S G S C A
M E R A S A C A M E R A S S H

page 105 • Got Cargo?

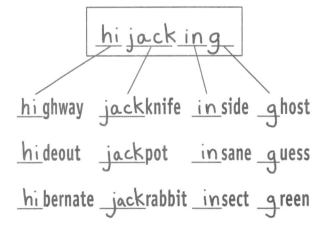

hijacking

highway   jackknife   inside   ghost

hideout   jackpot   insane   guess

hibernate   jackrabbit   insect   green

The Everything®

KIDS'
Series!

Packed with tons of information, activities, and puzzles, the Everything® Kids' books are perennial bestsellers that keep kids active and engaged.

Each book is two-color, 8" x 9¼", and 144 pages.

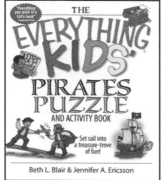

The Everything® Kids' Pirates
Puzzle and Activity Book
1-59337-607-3, $7.95

The Everything® Kids'
Horses Book
1-59337-608-1, $7.95

A silly, goofy, and undeniably icky addition to
the Everything® Kids' series . . .

The Everything® Kids'
GROSS
Series

Chock-full of sickening entertainment for hours of disgusting fun.

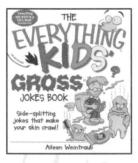

The Everything® Kids'
Gross Jokes Book
1-59337-448-8, $7.95

The Everything® Kids' Gross
Puzzle & Activity Book
1-59337-447-X, $7.95

The Everything® Kids'
Gross Mazes Book
1-59337-616-2, $7.95

The Everything® Kids' Gross
Hidden Pictures Book
1-59337-615-4, $7.95

Other Everything® Kids' Titles Available

All titles are $6.95 or $7.95 unless otherwise noted.

The Everything® Kids' Animal Puzzle & Activity Book
1-59337-305-8

The Everything® Kids' Baseball Book, 4th Ed.
1-59337-614-6

The Everything® Kids' Bible Trivia Book
1-59337-031-8

The Everything® Kids' Bugs Book
1-58062-892-3

The Everything® Kids' Christmas Puzzle &
Activity Book
1-58062-965-2

The Everything® Kids' Cookbook
1-58062-658-0

The Everything® Kids' Crazy Puzzles Book
1-59337-361-9

The Everything® Kids' Dinosaurs Book
1-59337-360-0

The Everything® Kids' Halloween Puzzle &
Activity Book
1-58062-959-8

The Everything® Kids' Hidden Pictures Book
1-59337-128-4

The Everything® Kids' Joke Book
1-58062-686-6

The Everything® Kids' Knock Knock Book
1-59337-127-6

The Everything® Kids' Math Puzzles Book
1-58062-773-0

The Everything® Kids' Mazes Book
1-58062-558-4

The Everything® Kids' Money Book
1-58062-685-8

The Everything® Kids' Nature Book
1-58062-684-X

The Everything® Kids' Puzzle Book
1-58062-687-4

The Everything® Kids' Riddles
& Brain Teasers Book
1-59337-036-9

The Everything® Kids' Science Experiments Book
1-58062-557-6

The Everything® Kids' Sharks Book
1-59337-304-X

The Everything® Kids' Soccer Book
1-58062-642-4

The Everything® Kids' Travel Activity Book
1-58062-641-6